DELICIOUS
DISSEMBLING

DELICIOUS DISSEMBLING

A Compleat Guide to Performing
Restoration Comedy

Suzanne M. Ramczyk

HEINEMANN
Portsmouth, NH

Heinemann

361 Hanover Street
Portsmouth, NH 03801–3912
www.heinemanndrama.com

Offices and agents throughout the world

Library of Congress Cataloging-in-Publication Data
Ramczyk, Suzanne M.
    Delicious dissembling : a compleat guide to performing restoration comedy / Suzanne M. Ramczyk.
        p. cm.
    Includes bibliographical references.
    ISBN 0-325-00375-0
    1. Acting.   2. English drama—Restoration, 1660–1700—History and criticism.   3. English drama (Comedy)—History and criticism.   I. Title.

PN2061 .R355   2002
792'. 028'094209032—dc21   2002001528

Editor: Lisa A. Barnett
Production: Elizabeth Valway
Cover design: Joni Doherty
Cover illustration: Jeanette de Jong
Interior illustrations: Jeanette de Jong and Arthur Dirks
Typesetter: TechBooks
Manufacturing: Jamie Carter

Printed in the United States of America on acid-free paper
T & C Digital 2009

CONTENTS

ACKNOWLEDGMENTS

I would like to thank my husband, Dr. Ed Zeldin, and my stepdaughter, Jordana, for their continued support and patience throughout the process of putting this book together. Thanks also to my contributors, Arthur Dirks, Jeanette de Jong, and Cynthia Blaise, and also to Gary Genard for his delightful suggestion.

INTRODUCTION

In this age of postmodernism and its corresponding deconstructed, reconstructed, and/or experimental theatrical production, at the core of any text addressing period style lies the question "Why should period style performance be studied?" In fact, such pedagogy is frequently ignored altogether. Beyond including a study of interpreting Shakespearean text, many theatre degree–granting institutions and conservatories provide little or no foundation in period style performance. Rather, they inculcate an acting style most suited for performing the genre of realism. Stanislavsky's work (as well as its many offshoots) partly accounts for this. Another major factor is the profound effect that television and film have had on the art of acting and on the theatre in general. There exist, of course, comprehensive theatre programs that embrace the study of period style, but there are many programs that do not have the resources or do not perceive the need to do so.

Although the plays of the Restoration and eighteenth-century England are not produced with the regularity of Shakespeare's texts, and one would be hard-pressed to find a festival devoted to the works of Congreve or Wycherley, for instance, these comedies are still frequently produced. *The Way of the World* and *The Country Wife*, as well as eighteenth-century plays that hearken back to the Restoration style (*The School for Scandal* and *She Stoops to Conquer*), are regularly a part of many professional, academic, community, and even high school theatre seasons. The ongoing mounting of these scintillating and bawdy Restoration (or Restoration-influenced) comedies attests to the great pleasure they are still capable of providing to modern audiences. Since these texts receive such frequent production, it follows that student actors should receive education in, or at least exposure to, the interpretation of the comedies of manners.

A likely retort to the claim that education in performing period style plays should be included in acting training might be that many companies do not produce these plays in their original historical context. Perhaps there have been in recent history as many modern settings of comedies of manners as there have been, for instance, of Shakespeare's *Macbeth*. So, again, why study period style if the plays are set in modern times and, furthermore, are being played to modern audiences? Several recent professional productions of Shakesperean and other period plays produced by highly esteemed American regional theatres may attest to this need. It seems there is a trend in much of the American theatre to rely on spectacle to "sell" the plays of any historical period to the theatregoing public. A regional theatre production of *Macbeth*, for instance, featured elaborate settings and costumes, with an astounding soundtrack accompanying the Scottish king's techno-nightmarish descent into bloody madness. However, much of the text was garbled or completely "lost," particularly by the actor in the title role. Although there were a few standout performances, several actors paid no attention to rhythm, operative words, and the variables of speech necessary to convey syntax and meaning. The production did not embrace the visceral and eloquent nature of Shakespeare's Elizabethan tragedy. A recent production of a Restoration comedy of manners featured breathtaking costumes, and belly laughs abounded. However, this production also downplayed the language, thereby sacrificing much of the playwright's witty dialogue and relying heavily on effects derived from farce, an entirely different genre. Perhaps both directors felt that these approaches, wherein the spoken text was quite subordinate to spectacle or physical comedy, could best assist in making the period plays accessible to contemporary audiences. In fact, many audience members had no difficulty in following the stories and the overall progression of character. Common responses included, "I don't know what they [the actors] were saying, but I understood the play," and "I didn't understand the lines, but I knew what was going on." While some might consider these comments complimentary to the productions, renderings of greater fidelity to the texts would effect a deeper appreciation and substantially enrich the audience's experience. Further, if the director of the mannered comedy had more conscientiously delineated the characters' physical lives inherent in the play, rather than relying on farcical movement, comprehension may have been better served.

Beyond any consideration of the importance of textual intelligibility, the plays of historical periods are typically founded on the societal concerns, sensibility, and aesthetics that governed all modes of human interaction in their times. With respect to the comedies of manners, the genre itself ridicules, parodies, or satirizes the social behavior of a stratum of society in a particular era. They highlight and ridicule such societal concerns as the necessity for a keen verbal wit, the fastidious execution of a myriad of articles of deportment and manners, and the arranging of liaisons. Further, it was a small court coterie that concerned themselves with these social details. Thus, because at the very core of these comedies is a focus on the values and aesthetics of a specific group of people in a specific time period, it is difficult to overlook these considerations in modern resettings. For instance, if language, wit in particular, lies at the very core of a play, a major question might be "Why produce the play if one has no desire to feature language?" If holding up manners and deportment to scrutiny or ridicule was the main intent of the playwright, how can the period's physical concerns be overlooked altogether?

That is not to say that Restoration comedies of manners, or those of any period for that matter, will not succeed if set in modern times. Rather, I propose that a comprehensive understanding of the values, aesthetics, and focus of a play's time period and of the playwright will enhance the impact of any modern resetting. With such a foundation, the director, designers, and actors can make informed choices about translating historical concerns into modern times. Perhaps the director may have to confront the ultimate question of "Can (or should) this play be set in contemporary times?" For example, the high comedies of the Restoration are focused around what we might call *externals* today. The inner lives of the characters, with which we are so fascinated in this post-Stanislavskian era, were not of any concern to the Restoration lady or gentleman, nor, therefore, to the Restoration playwright. As theatre practitioners, perhaps we must ask ourselves if, in fact, a play that centers on external behavior and deportment can be reset in the twenty-first century and the audiences be expected to relate. Or, perhaps, an appropriate question is whether or not there is any correlation in our time to such a focus on external behavior. Again, an understanding of the sensibilities of both the era and of the playwrights in the era will assist in answering these questions.

To be sure, not all contemporary productions of period style are reset into modern times. Many recent productions of plays from many different periods at major regional theatres in North America have been set in more historically correct contexts. Additionally, many colleges and universities have embraced the need to expose their students to productions of period plays set in their appropriate historical contexts. As suggested earlier, some of these programs are well equipped to deal with all aspects of producing and performing Restoration comedies and other period plays, with the necessary staff to teach voice and text work, movement requirements, and acting considerations. Others, however, may be lacking in one or more of these areas because of the size or focus of their programs. As a respondent for many years for the Kennedy Center American College Theatre Festival, I have often been called upon to respond to period plays, particularly those of the seventeenth and eighteenth centuries. I have witnessed a gamut of interpretation, understanding, and facility in performance and production. There have been *Way of the Worlds* set in the early eighteenth century with absolutely no concern paid to the execution of the artificial speech. There have been *Marriage of Figaros* in which the actors moved their bodies about the stage as any healthy, pop-nurtured twenty-year-old would in this century and country. There have been many Restoration comedies and comedies of

Moliere in which the actors were lavishly dressed in sumptuous period costuming, but their voices and bodies clearly belonged to our time. Productions such as these are merely contemporary performances in fancy dress.

Finally, in recommending that a study of period style performance, and of the Restoration comedies of manners in particular, be included in a course of study, two strong contentions can be made. First, since the language of the texts is rooted in wit and artifice, a study of the plays can expose the actor to structure, syntax, and a myriad of literary and dramatic devices that is not possible through a study of contemporary comedy. In fact, for the training of actors in the English-speaking theatre, these comedies afford some of the best available material for handling the nuances of artifice-laden language. Second, these texts provide a wonderful basis for embracing a study of high comedy. In today's world, with the immense popularity of sitcoms and sitcom-inspired plays, it is easy to forget—or for a young actor to be ignorant of the fact—that not all comedy through the ages was of the low type.

This book, then, is written to answer a threefold need. First, for theatre programs that wish to include a study of performing the style of Restoration comedies of manners, this book may serve as a text that covers all aspects of performance. The major areas of study, addressing textual analysis, the voice as an interpreter of the text, the necessary physical considerations, and the acting, are analyzed. Exercises, short passages, and short scenes are provided to be used in the classroom or studio. Second, the book may also function as a handbook for production for companies wishing to mount Restoration comedies of manners. For the director who finds herself without assistance in any of the areas of text, voice, and physical work, the book will provide comprehensive discussion and practical approaches to these areas. For a director who finds himself lacking support or expertise in only one area, the book may also prove helpful. I should note that the book may also be useful when producing the works of Sheridan and Goldsmith, particularly with respect to the use of language. To varying degrees, both playwrights were very influenced by the writers of the Restoration and, in disdain for the rise of Sentimentalism, attempted to recapture the scintillating dialogue of that former era. Third, the book will also prove helpful to an actor who finds himself cast in one of the plays and has little, no, or only cursory training or knowledge of the genre.

The book may serve another ancillary function, particularly for voice and text analysis courses. Since these comedies possess some of the most artificial, witty, and sparkling language ever to grace the stages of the English-speaking theatre, Chapters 3 and 4, focusing on the analysis of the devices of speech and the vocal interpretation of these devices, may offer a foundation for the study and performance of artifice-laden speech.

The book is arranged around the following major topics: Chapter 1 provides a brief historical overview of the period, the plays and playwrights, the theatre, and the most notable actors of the time. Chapter 2 addresses two major concerns or problems that the contemporary actor often faces when performing period style plays, that of reconciling Stanislavsky-based training with an acting style not founded in realism, and that of confronting a style based in *externals*. Approaches and exercises are provided to assist in this process. The major types of Restoration characters are introduced, as well as several components of the overall sensibility of the age. Exercises illuminate these concepts. Chapter 3 introduces the student to the major components, devices, and stylistic concerns of the language, as well as the main topics and sensibilities addressed within the texts. Excerpts from the plays and exercises demonstrate and afford practice in these components of text. Chapter 4 utilizes the textual analysis of the preceding chapter as a springboard for practical vocal interpretive application. It includes a study of *operative words*, utilizes Laban's theories of movement as an approach toward interpreting and bringing meaning to the texts, explains and demonstrates the use of the *vocal variables of speech* to illuminate text, and provides many excerpts and exercises for practice. Chapter 5 addresses the physical components of performing these comedies, which are rooted in the physical aesthetic, the deportment, the manners, the fashion, and other concerns of the period. Major trends in fashion are described; sensibilities are delineated; components of Laban are utilized as interpretive tools; bows, curtsies, the use of the fan, and snuff taking, as well as many other types of movement and gesture are delineated; all movement is broken down into its component parts; and exercises, with and without text, are provided.

At the conclusion of each chapter, the same scene from William Congreve's *Way of the World* is analyzed from the perspective of the main topics covered within the respective chapters. Interpretive choices are also provided. These analyses are included to demonstrate practical application of the components covered, as well as to provide examples of possible performative choices.

Finally, this book was written to celebrate one of the most dazzling types of comedy that has emerged in the English-speaking theatre, the Restoration comedies of manners, in hope that it may assist theatre educators to instill in their students a zest for language, a joyous appreciation of the brilliant linguistic sensibility that lies at the core of the genre, and a love for playing artifice and manners—that which lies at the heart of all high comedy.

DELICIOUS DISSEMBLING

1

OVERVIEW: A BRIEF HISTORY
OF RESTORATION ENGLAND

May 29, 1660, was a momentous day in English history and in the history of English-speaking theatre as well. Amidst celebration, the likes of which London may never have seen before, King Charles II entered London after eleven years of exile. On this day—the day of his thirtieth birthday—tapestries hung in great profusion from windows. Flags flew on high, church bells rang, and lords and nobles turned out in their finery. Wine even flowed from fountains. Parliament ordered May 29 forever to be regarded a day of thanksgiving for England's redemption from tyranny. After the imposed austerity of the Commonwealth, the sovereign's return to England heralded a return to a long-denied elegant lifestyle for society's elite. With the restoration of the monarchy, the "polite world," in particular, enjoyed an array of amenities and freedoms that perhaps surpassed long-suppressed wishes. The genteel set could find newly imported luxuries in shops and once again concern itself with the minutest details of deportment and social manners. Children could once more engage in games and sports long denied by the Puritans. Composers relished their newfound freedom, no longer restricted to composing within the confines of church music. Patents were issued whereby the theatres were officially reopened; actors flourished in their art, no longer carrying the stigma of godless and frivolous people. Probably because of his exposure to women onstage in Paris, the king allowed for the use of actresses onstage, a practice that was eagerly embraced by Restoration theatrical producers and audiences alike. Playwrights indulged in the

1

now-respectable pastime of playwriting, contributing some of the finest artificial comedies in the English language.

However, it was not merely the reestablishment of the monarchy in general that freed England from the yoke of drabness and denial, but rather the restoration of Charles II in particular. It was Charles' manners, as well as his likes, dislikes, and behavior, that afforded particularly the upper tiers of society a liberated, stylish, and sparkling new lifestyle. Certainly Charles' experiences at the French court influenced Restoration court life. Additionally, his many adventures, hardships, and experiences in other countries during his exile played an important role in shaping the new king's court. Further, an important influence on his very early life was the Earl of Newcastle, into whose care he was entrusted at the age of eight. Newcastle was the first of his governors, and the only one to have any profound impact on shaping the future king's behavior. He instilled his pupil with the need for good manners, to be demonstrated particularly toward great people and women. Scholarship was not encouraged but sportsmanship was, and the qualities of a true gentleman were paramount to Newcastle's teachings.

Charles was sixteen when he left England for France. Because of the increasing unrest in England in 1646, young Charles went to France to live modestly for a while with his mother, and he enjoyed such popular pastimes as conducting scientific experiments, studying mathematics with Hobbes, as well as making the rounds of balls, plays, and masques. In 1648 a Parliamentary fleet turned itself over to the Royalists and Charles felt the possibility to take action against Cromwell's growing power. Charles hurried to the Dutch authorities, seeking their intervention. But within a short time, Charles I was beheaded and young Charles' plans were necessarily changed. He started for Ireland to commence a campaign against Cromwell, but after Cromwell's own ruthless campaign there, Charles changed his plans and embarked on a misguided trip to Scotland. There, his court was a mere mockery, and he was allowed no input into affairs pertaining to thwarting Cromwell. Cromwell readily marched into and defeated Scotland. Charles escaped the retreating Scottish army (which kept him under close scrutiny) and returned to his homeland, where for weeks he was a hunted fugitive. When he finally escaped back to France, Charles had accumulated enough adventure and wondrous stories with which to entertain for the remainder of his life.

Once again in the French court, Charles and his entourage had to make the best of poverty. Under constant besiege from creditors and as court morale worsened, Charles enthusiastically indulged in those pleasures to which he was previously accustomed, including singing, dancing, and engaging in numerous liaisons for which he was already notorious. The conditions of the struggling court became more and more impoverished and Mazarin expelled Charles and his followers to wander about Europe. Spending their time in the towns of southern Germany, Charles' court seemed not to suffer, still often enjoying the feasting and balls to which they had become accustomed. It is noteworthy that one aspect of Charles' banished court that was to eventually become a hallmark of his Restoration court was thoroughly documented by Cromwellian spies. One noted:

> I think I may truly say that greater abominations were never practiced among people than at this day at Charles Stuart's court. Fornication, drunkenness and adultery are esteemed no sins amongst them.[1]

In 1655, Charles spent time in Flanders, then Spanish territory, to enlist the Spanish to engage with the Royalists against Cromwell. Then in 1658, from the time of Cromwell's death, Charles moved to Calais to ready himself for his imminent return. Finally, after Cromwell's son failed to keep the Commonwealth together at a time when Parliament and the army were at odds, England was once again cheered by the thought of the return to a monarchy. Charles was sent for.

THE COURT AND WORLD OF CHARLES II

When studying the plays of the Restoration and the habits of the polite world, it is easy for one to accumulate a limited, somewhat lopsided picture of seventeenth-century London and England in general. The elegance of court-oriented life readily overshadows the bleaker, or at least dirtier, background. For example, when studying the manners of genteel men and women of the seventeenth century, one learns that when two people were walking, the "wall side" of the street must always be offered to the person of higher social standing or to a lady. This practice was not rooted in some artificial details of deportment; rather, it was rooted in a very practical concern. Slop pots were regularly emptied from second story windows or balconies. A balcony overhang could offer substantial protection, as could one's nearness to a wall in the absence of a balcony, when slop was being flung from a window overhead. This practice, which in light of modern sanitation we find quite shocking, is only one component of life within an environment much more visceral than the more sterile one associated with the developed countries of the twenty-first century. Because of the lack of public sanitation, rivers of sludge and filth generally flowed down the streets of Restoration London. Heavy clouds of smoke and vapors generated by dyers and brewers hung over the city. Stalls scattered all around the city added to the stench of the streets. Insects and vermin were in abundance, as were outbreaks of small pox, fevers of many varieties, and the plague.

However, amidst this backdrop, a new, colorful world emerged, particularly in London. The sparkling court life spawned by Charles renewed a splendor long denied to society's upper crust. Fashionable people strolled the streets in a variegated array of sparkling and shimmering garments. Shops, now inventoried with the goods long desired by those who could afford luxury, added to the color and splendor of the previously gray streets. Additionally, entertainment ranging from cockfighting, bear baiting, and socializing in alehouses to the amenities offered by chocolate shops, coffeehouses, and the theatre added a *joie de vivre* previously denied the city for several years. It was a world of sharp contrasts, but one of vitality, exuberance, and color!

As suggested earlier, Charles himself was very much responsible for the reinstatement of luxurious living for the leisured class. The king was indeed the arbiter of all things fashionable among the elite set. He was the leader in fashionable clothing; he was an avid dancer, an enthusiastic sportsman who played tennis and rode horses, and a regular patron of the theatre.

Charles' guiding principles of deportment were rooted in a sense of ease. A gentleman was required to be at ease with himself and to put others at ease. It was felt that the old manners of England were exceedingly rough and boisterous; the new king's court took a more civil view on social discourse. Disputing theology and undertaking any argument at the table were deemed to be low. Indeed, to be earnest in anything was frowned upon. True sentiment and emotion were to be cloaked or masked by civility: a gentle or convivial air, elegant language and wit, and elegant bearing. Fashionable manners were learned and cultivated from the time of childhood, and guidebooks containing rules for civility proliferated. In fact, such books and the training provided by a dance master were indispensable, as the rules governing the myriad articles of deportment and social interaction reached a high degree of artificial complexity. This complex code of manners dictated such particulars as how to take snuff, use a fan, bow, curtsy, stand, sit, walk, loll in a carriage, stroll in the park, and drink chocolate. Thus, it took many years of concerted study in order for one to appear "at ease."

Court life was truly at the center of life for the polite set. Not only did Charles' court define fashion and fashionable manners for the privileged, but the court was also very much a public place. The affairs of state were not cloaked in mystery but were truly public property. The king dined in state while the fashionable world promenaded and relished the pageantry from the galleries. Set among a spectacle of trumpeters and drummers in scarlet hues, royal servants served on bended knee. The public was also free to view many royal entertainments and balls from the galleries at

Whitehall. The famous contemporary diarist Samuel Pepys documents many such viewings. In December of 1662, he notes how he viewed an audience with the Russian ambassador from a high gallery. He comments on the splendor and notes the gifts that were presented, including "rich furs, hawkes, carpets, cloths of tissue, and seahorse teethe." He continues, "The King took two or three hawkes upon his fist, having a glove on, wrought with gold, given him for that purpose."[2]

It was no surprise that with the monarchy restored, the pursuit of idle pleasures—including sexual pleasures—was a favored pastime for courtiers and a favorite topic for playwrights. The king's licentious behavior, which had previously been thoroughly documented during his exile, did not alter. Pepys did not mince his words when commenting on such activities, noting that on August 31, 1661, things at court were in "very ill condition," there being so much "swearing, drinking, and whoring."[3] The king was notorious for his innumerable liaisons. His chief mistress over the years was Lady Castlemaine, with whom he fathered at least five children. However, he did not confine his attentions to her and his wife. He favored actresses, daughters of the clergy, and even waiting women. The famous actresses Moll Davies and Nell Gwynne were among his many consorts, Nell remaining a favorite to the end of his life. He was generous to all and to his many children. The public display of affection in court was certainly not discouraged, the lead being taken from the king himself. Additionally, his own courtiers were usually quite lax in their manners with the monarch. Although Charles apparently did not indulge heavily in such vices, drinking, swearing, and gambling were not discouraged in his court.

Charles' pastimes, however, were not confined to the joys of dissipation. The king was an ardent fan of the theatre, and with his restoration, the theatres were officially reopened. The king issued licenses to William Davenant and Thomas Killigrew, effectively granting them a monopoly on theatrical production. Patents were also eventually granted to touring and provincial companies. Charles was responsible for the theatre's rebirth, which fostered some of the most coruscating comedies ever to dazzle the English-speaking stage. Poet Laureate John Dryden, who wrote predominantly dramas, was a favorite of the king's. But the king's appetite for French fashion and his intolerance for boredom at the theatre led to a profusion of bawdy and supremely witty comedies of manners. Charles did not object to licentious wit off or on the stage, and playwrights vied to cater to the appetite of the king and court. No longer were they quashed by the censorship of the Puritans, but rather propelled by the inclinations of the newly restored monarchy.

PLAYS AND PLAYWRIGHTS

The plays of the period were typically framed by the brighter, gayer world of the elite class, not the visceral one associated with the common man. The playwrights themselves were members of the polite world and, thus, wrote plays that were set in, plotted on the activities of, and reflected the people of the world in which they moved. They concerned themselves with material that would interest and suit the tastes of a small aristocratic court coterie. Thus, although a rising merchant class was beginning to populate the theatre, it is safe to say that the plays were basically written for, about, and by the inhabitants of a court-oriented society.

In spite of the narrow focus of the playwrights and the monopolies established with the king's patents, playwriting flourished. In the period between 1660 and 1700, more than four hundred known plays were written by no less than 180 playwrights. The king's favorite, and probably the most versatile of the Restoration playwrights, contributed to the developing genre of comedy of manners in addition to his more serious plays. Dryden (1631–1700) firmly established the convention of a pair of witty, carefree, upper-class lovers with his *Sir Martin Mar-All, The Mock Astrologer*, and *Marriage a la Mode*. However, Sir George Etherege (1634–1691) is credited with establishing several of the typical components of comedies of manners after experimenting with the form in *Love in a Tub*. In *She Would if She Could*, and *The Man of Mode*, the characters concern themselves with liaisons, seduction, necessary marriages, and the latest fashions, all while engaging in witty repartee. William Wycherley (1640–1715) provided his brilliant, funniest, and still often produced satire *The Country Wife*. Additionally, he penned the sardonic *Love in a Wood* and *The Gentleman Dancing Master* and the brutal satire *The Plain Dealer*. Typically, William Congreve is credited with bringing the form to its most sparkling pinnacle. His clearly drawn characters, dazzling dialogue, rapier wit, biting satire, and brilliant depiction of sex antagonism account for his often-bestowed appellation as the greatest writer of English comedy. His *Way of the World* is still one of the most often produced Restoration plays. His other works include *The Old Batchelour, The Double Dealer*, and *Love for Love*.

Two other playwrights should also be considered: Sir John Vanbrugh and George Farquhar. Vanbrugh is often accused of pilfering from the more notable playwrights of the period and of lacking in any real vision. Farquhar is often evaluated in light of his movement away from the sparkling comedies, embracing sentimentalism and domestic comedy. However, both writers incorporated many attributes of the comedies of manners, most notably the use of witty dialogue. Vanbrugh's works include *The Relapse, The Provok'd Wife*, and *The Confederacy*. Farquhar contributed *The Constant Couple; or A Trip to the Jubilee, The Twin Rivals, The Recruiting Officer,* and *The Beaux' Stratagem.*

These playwrights, who were all members of the polite world (some, in fact, were courtiers), wrote some of the most self-conscious plays in the history of English theatre. Their works focused on the tastes of a quite homogenous audience, whose interests and concerns included the pursuit of idle pleasures, the love chase, the honing of witty language and dialogue, an infatuation with all things fashionable, the necessity of marriage, the extrication of oneself from a no longer desirable entanglement, and the proper execution of the complex code of manners. Logically, the characters in these comedies are predominantly denizens of the Restoration charmed circle. For the most part, the playwrights did not concern themselves with the lower types that liberally populate much of Elizabethan comedy. The major characters are aristocrats by birth and are typically wealthy, cynical, and amorous. Ancillary characters include some country gulls and a few less colorful citizens, with some bawds thrown in for further color and titillation. This sense of self-consciousness is also revealed through the plays' settings. Playwrights were quite audacious in placing their plays in locations readily identifiable to their audience. Aristocratic drawing rooms, St. James Park, Hyde Park, Mulberry Gardens, and other fashionable meeting places typically provided the backdrops for the action. All in all, the playwrights, who were very much a part of the elite genteel circle, wrote plays that catered in every way to the appetites of their audiences.

THE THEATRE, ITS ACTORS, AND AUDIENCES

Not only did the playwrights pen comedies to suit the tastes of a small court coterie, but the theatres themselves also contributed to the self-consciousness and a keen sense of intimacy. As noted earlier, the king granted licenses to Killigrew and Davenant, who eventually established the King's Theatre at Drury Lane and the Duke of York's at Lincoln's Inn. To visualize these theatres, one must imagine something quite different from the physical plants of today's theatre. First, the separation between audience and actor was not so pronounced as in most modern houses. Generally, actors performed on the forestage in front of painted scenery. Only general lighting was used that did not distinguish the actors' space from that of the audience. Audiences were crowded into a very small house, and seating was available on the stage itself. Pepys, an avid theatregoer, documented and complained many times of the overcrowding in the theatres. In 1667, he noted that the King's Theatre was "so full as I never saw it, I was forced to stand all the while close to the very door, till I took cold, and many people went away for want of room."[4] As far as Pepys was concerned, this crowding was as much a part of the changing demographics of the audiences as it was the size of the theatres. Throughout his journals, he frequently complained about this change, which more and more included doctors, lawyers, parliamentarians, administrators, writers, merchants, and the wives of such.

The overall experience of the audience was also quite removed from what one generally experiences in modern times. The crowded conditions contributed to an atmosphere that would be intolerable by today's standards. The pervasive fumes from the many candles and the closeness of the latrines, combined with the presence of so many unwashed bodies, would provide a remarkably challenging experience, even for the most ardent theatre enthusiast of modern times. The mere presence of women in the audience, particularly the orange girls and the ladies of the town, vied with the stage action for the audience's attention. The behavior of the audience was anything but quiet and respectful, with a lack of decorum unimaginable to today's audiences. Citizens and gallants alike were known to cry out, whistle, clap, talk back to the actors, hiss when they disapproved of the action onstage, haggle with the orange girls, and even jump onto the stage. At times, the men would break into loud jests or song, and at others, swords were drawn and the play brought to a halt. However, lest we judge the Restoration audiences too harshly, it is necessary to understand that most of this behavior was expected and was indicative of a degree of intimacy between audience and actors that is unknown to modern theatregoers. Finally, the intimacy extended beyond that which could be achieved during a performance, as favored patrons were known to regularly visit the actors—particularly their female favorites—in their rooms backstage.

A liberal use of music also contributed to the overall theatregoing experience. A small orchestra or consort accompanied every production. Seated in an overhead gallery, the musicians played overtures and accompanied the many songs, dances, and jigs that were inserted into most every play. Music and dance also provided additional entertainment between acts.

The actor-audience relationship spawned an acting style that did not rely on illusion-based theatre. Indeed, a theatre based on a strong sense of illusion was nearly impossible; the spectator was always aware of the theatrical fact. Actors eagerly played into the world of the audience, easily engaging it through full asides, prologues, and epilogues. Actors delivered their lines as much to the audience as to other actors. Finally, within the relatively small confines of the theatres, the actors could rely on minute gestures to subtly convey subtext and innuendo.

Truly, the Restoration engendered an actor's theatre, led by such luminaries as James Nokes, Cave Underhill, Henry Harris, William

Mountfort, John Lacy, and the renowned Thomas Betterton. For many (if not most) patrons, however, it was truly an actress' theatre, led by the likes of Nell Gwynn, Moll Davies, Elizabeth Barry, and Ann Bracegirdle. In fact, the major theatrical innovation of the times was the introduction of women onstage, a practice that can also be attributed to the king. Clearly, Charles had been entertained by the sight of women on the stage during his exile. When criticized for his leniency, he defended his stand that women should play female roles because it was more offensive for men to dress as women onstage than for women to display themselves in public. Women became indispensable to the stage as they lured audiences with their good looks and their charms, producers taking full advantage by exploiting their most visible assets. Occasions were found by which the women's shoulders and décolletage were readily displayed, such as through a deep curtsy. Dancing and dressing in a nightgown offered further occasion to flaunt an actress' charms. Finally, the new practice of dressing women in breeches was a favorite manner by which a woman's legs could be displayed. These "breeches" roles also offered opportunity for fondling by the male actors.

SUMMARY

All in all, Restoration England was a period of tremendous exuberance. Loosed from the yoke of Puritanism, all levels of society were free to enjoy long-denied pleasures and opportunities. With Charles II's return from exile amidst great pomp and splendor, the upper tiers of society, in particular, were eager to indulge in many of the pastimes and practices so readily embraced by the king in all his travels. Although it certainly cannot be said that the king's exile was a completely happy and comfortable one, once restored, Charles created a court life and court-oriented society informed by both his more genteel encounters and his own hedonistic nature. French manners and fashion were key influences on the polite world, as were the monarch's own more lusty sensibilities. Society became consumed with the minutest details of deportment, the innuendo of movement, and physical attitude. Dancing masters were required from the time of childhood, and handbooks for deportment and civility were now readily available. The aristocratic ease in bearing flaunted by the king and court was carefully honed, governed, as it was, by a myriad of rules of deportment. Mastery of the proper articles of good breeding afforded access to a world of licentiousness, which among the upper class was taken for granted.

Although it cannot be claimed that the period spawned a people's theatre, plays and playwriting flourished, catering to an elite audience and engendering one of the most self-conscious genres in the history of English-speaking theatre. Perhaps the most vibrant form to arise from this period is the sparkling comedy of manners, whose playwrights held up a fun house mirror to the pleasure-loving and idle court-oriented society. Additionally, the era gave rise to one of the most intimate types of theatrical production in history, with the physical space, the behavior and makeup of the audiences, the plays themselves, and the actors all conspiring to engender this close relationship.

NOTES

1. Quoted in Christopher Falkus, *The Life and Times of Charles II* (Garden City, NY: Doubleday, 1972), p. 54.
2. Robert Latham, *The Shorter Pepys* (Berkeley: University of California Press, 1985), p. 244.
3. Ibid., p. 151.
4. Ibid., p. 756.

2

SOME BASIC ACTING CONCERNS

INTRODUCTION

When initially approaching the acting of Restoration comedies of manners, there emerge two problems or considerations that actors often confront. The first is a concern arising out of the manner in which the plays were originally performed. Because modern-day actors are so firmly rooted in a performance style defined by the early authors of realism, such as Chekhov and Ibsen, and in the teachings and theories of Stanislavski, a historical style that seemingly defies *fourth-wall realism* can pose many concerns. Next, the more important consideration a post-Stanislavskian actor must embrace is discovering a means by which one may reconcile the acting of texts based so firmly in external behavior with modern approaches to and assumptions about acting.

The first consideration is usually quite easily addressed. The concern stems from the fact that the comedies originally found expression in the intimate and boisterous surroundings of the Restoration playhouse, with the playwrights capitalizing on these conditions. Actors, performing in front of scenery, indulged in an intimacy with their audiences to a degree rarely achieved again in the history of the theatre. The close proximity of actor to spectator and an absence of stage lighting allowed exchanges whereby a wink, a tossing of the head, or a slight nod could convey a myriad of nonverbal messages to the audience. Additionally, the fact that playgoers went to the theatre to see themselves, as well as those members of their coterie who were not quite as successful as they in moving

11

through such an artifice-laden code of social behavior, re-created on-stage contributed to a sense of identification. The audience members were clearly watching themselves! This sort of intimacy is impossible in modern-day productions of these comedies.

One can readily glean that this intimacy forged a style of acting in which the fourth wall was not a concern. Prologues, epilogues, and full asides, as well as the practice of leading actors playing fully to their audiences, suggest a highly presentational style. Even if the prologues, epilogues, and asides are considered acceptable conventions today, the distinct playing to the audience would be perceived as far too presentational for the tastes of modern Western audiences, who are accustomed to a more hypnotic tension between the audience and actors. The plays assumed this high degree of audience interaction and the actors reveled in the presentational style. Clearly, today, no audience can relate to the characters and action of a Restoration comedy from a perspective of viewing themselves onstage. The people and behaviors presented, and often mocked, are far removed from the experience of any theatregoer of the twenty-first century. Further, modern stage lighting, scenery, and stage mechanics do not typically allow for a lack of separation between audience and actor. Even when a Restoration facility and stage design are approximated, the same sort of intimacy is unattainable. Thus, the most common and most effective approach to any concerns of a historical style is to maintain the direct audience address through the conventions of the asides, prologues, and epilogues, and to embrace a more modern approach for the performance of the majority of the text.

The second, and by far the more important, concern arises out of the need to reconcile the externally focused behavior portrayed in the comedies with an internally focused modern acting style. At the heart of Restoration comedies of manners is what we would consider today to be *externals*. That is, the comedies were written to reflect the behavior, values, and sensibilities of a small elite segment of society in Restoration England. The plays celebrate this court-oriented society's infatuation with highly adorned, well-honed language, with fashionable clothing, with the game and chase of love, and with a complex code of decorum, manners, and physical bearing. In this polite world, whose denizens were quite obsessed with outward appearance, it was believed that one's manners reflected the authentic or inner person. The inhabitants were not concerned with the ability to express oneself in any deep or psychologically meaningful way. Indeed, such a practice would surely be frowned upon. Rather, to converse in an artful or clever manner was considered a necessary social skill. Emotion was masked or cloaked in beautiful language; an artful voice delivered this artifice-laden speech; physical bearing was studied and calculated to present an elegant physical picture; and a primary function of clothing or fashion was to provide the opportunity for display or flaunting. The comedies celebrated this infatuation with externals to such an extent that character in these plays can be viewed as merely the vehicle for a resplendent display of manners. The lack of psychological complexity is reflected in the practice of naming characters such that their names define their overall drive, failing, or predominant trait or attribute. The plays reverberate with the likes of Witwoud, Loveless, Ranger, Lord and Lady Froth, Horner, Flirt, Dapperwit, Petulant, Mrs. Sullen, Squeamish, Lady Townley, Pinchwife, Manly, and Mrs. Dainty Fidget.

In modern times, most actors have been steeped in approaches to acting the genre of realism that focus on methods of embracing the inner psychological lives of characters, seemingly in stark contrast to the display of externals celebrated in the Restoration comedies. That is, it is often perceived as difficult, or even impossible, to embrace all the external concerns of the comedies while attempting to maintain a sense of inner psychological truth. Since these comedies are produced today under very different social and theatrical conditions, and since they are interpreted by actors steeped in acting training and/or traditions far removed from that associated with the Restoration stage, the problems or concerns outlined here must be confronted in terms of a melding. The demands of the inherent style and sensibilities within the plays must somehow be wedded with the acting and production styles of modern Western theatre and the sensibilities of its audiences.

In order to commence a reconciliation of modern acting practice with the style concerns associated with this period, it is imperative that *artifice* is not confused with *artificial* in the contemporary sense of *inauthentic*. It is quite common for the inexperienced actor of period style to view the characters to be "fake" or "phony." Herein, a realignment of thinking must occur. First and foremost, the desires, goals, pursuits, or drives of the characters in the comedies are as real and as authentic as any that impel more modern characters. Many of these drives are quite similar, in fact. Not only characters of Restoration comedy strive to achieve the love of or a liaison with a beloved, attempt to extricate themselves from a failed love relationship, seek to impress others within a social group, or simply desire to relish the joys of youth or good health. Although the characters are painted rather broadly and may not concern themselves with intense psychological outpourings or ignite what today we would consider emotionally charged confrontations, their desires or *objectives* are as true to life as any found in more contemporary texts, as well as in human behavior. It is at this level of humanity and truthfulness that the characters must initially be embraced.

Next, there is the major concern of how to deal with all the artifice-laden physical, textual, and vocal expression. How can there be any sincerity or truthfulness behind a much-studied bow and a well-turned phrase? Further, many an actor new to period style will view these behaviors as something separate from the more internal work of defining objectives. They may approach these behaviors as something to be added to or layered on top of the inner drive of a character. Additionally, many actors initially respond to these socially prescribed behaviors as something that will restrict their acting. Rather, the bows and curtsies, using the fan and snuff taking, and the beautifully constructed phrases, along with the vocal facility to deliver them, are all part and parcel of the communication of one's desires. That is, these external behaviors, so foreign to modern-day actors, are the means by which Restoration inhabitants of the polite set, and thus the characters in the comedies, attempted to attain their desires or objectives. Further, all denizens of the upper social stratum had the common goal of wanting to be perceived as true gentlemen and ladies. Since the authentic man or woman was judged by his or her outer bearing, all had a common underlying goal of attempting to maintain the standing as a true denizen of the polite world. Thus, many of the details of deportment can be viewed, for instance, as the means by which the characters pursue their goals of winning at the game of love or as ways of impressing someone else with their social ease and grace.[1] The fan work becomes a means by which a woman may attract a man; the carefully timed similitude or epigram may be used to convince an elder of one's true quality. Finally, many actors come to realize that the carefully prescribed behaviors offer a sense of freedom. That is, once the socially ordained behaviors are learned, an actor is never at a loss for what to do with his voice or his body.

It follows, then, that the work associated with attaining the proper physical and vocal masks, as well as embracing the language and textual concerns, should be approached with a clear sense of achieving objectives. Further, if no other acting or character objectives are apparent, the objectives of merely impressing someone or of flaunting one's behavior will always suffice for the purposes of any acting etude. Additionally, rather than seeking some deep, psychologically motivated drive, an overall objective will often be suggested by a character's name.

Since the external behavior is at the heart of acting the comedies, this chapter will provide only an introduction to several major values or sensibilities of Restoration society that are mirrored in the plays and must be manifested in the work of the actor. Thus, these topics and exercises will provide an overview to the more detailed acting work to be delineated in the subsequent chapters addressing the texts of the comedies, the utilization of the voice to illuminate the text, and the movement and physical considerations. Short scenes will be included to demonstrate overall social sensibilities and to allow the actor to experiment with expressing the basic underlying values of the stratum of society reflected in the plays. Further, the exercises will serve as etudes to allow the actor to commence a way of thinking that embraces the considerations of melding period style with modern acting methods. Culminating the chapter, a scene from William Congreve's *Way of the World* will be briefly discussed in light of general stylistic acting concerns, and will then provide the basis for further analysis at the conclusion of the three subsequent chapters.

CHARACTER TYPES

Before moving into the actual acting work of this chapter, it is important to understand the three classifications of character types that are created in the comedies, which reflect how the privileged class of Restoration society viewed people in its world. There are three general categories of characters: the *true wits*, the *false wits*, and the *witless*. The true wits (often referred to simply as the *wits*) are those gentlemen and ladies who are successful in presenting the socially prescribed, artful mask of the polite world. These characters are accomplished in the physical manners and deportment and adept in the required verbal dexterity, and have achieved in all outward manifestation a sense of elegant ease. The second category is that of the false wits, who have also studied and honed the numerous details of social deportment and who can practice these with as much skill as the true wits, but who often go too far in the execution of their manners. They are the slaves to all things fashionable, excess being their hallmark. This group is also often referred to as the *fops*, who can be either young or old. The final group is the witless, or the poor unfortunates who can only aspire to true wit and manners. Typically, these are not true inhabitants of the elite set, either because of circumstance or by choice; however, there are exceptions. The following discussions and exercises will deal primarily with achieving the style of the true wits, as it is their behavior that lies at the core of performing the comedies. The style of the false wits can readily be achieved through a sense of "going too far," and the creation of character for the witless will not be addressed, as these characters are devoid of the necessary decorum and deportment and, thus, lack the basic requisite sensibilities. Ongoing suggestions will be made for interpreting the exercises from the perspective of the false wits.

ACHIEVING OBJECTIVES THROUGH EXTERNALS

As discussed earlier, all the external behavior associated with the Restoration gentlemen and women can be viewed in acting terms as the means by which a character seeks to achieve his objectives. Since this premise is at the core of approaching the acting of the comedies, what follows is a series of exercises designed to allow the actor to experiment with this concept. Additionally, since the codes of behavior in Restoration society were determined by the upper tier of society, several of the following exercises will require the use of various behaviors that are predetermined by the class or the studio group at large. The group will be defining physical and vocal vocabularies for communication, in order that the actor may experiment with communication, or her struggle to achieve her goals, through preordained, socially mandated behaviors. Remember, it is not so important to actually achieve your desired objective in any given exercise as it is to attempt to succeed in your goal.

Exercises

Making Faces

Sit or stand facing a partner or a group of people. Experiment with arousing different responses from the other person or the group by making a variety of faces. Experiment with different ways of smiling, frowning, and just mugging in general.

Sound Objectives

Similar to the previous exercise, utilize another person or a group to elicit a variety of predetermined responses by experimenting with sound. Avoiding actual words altogether, use different English phonemes, as well as any vocal sounds you can generate.

Communicating Corporeally

Continue in the manner outlined in the two previous exercises, this time utilizing broader gesture and movement. You may choose to focus initially on the gesture of one appendage, and continue by adding on others. For example, attempt to achieve an objective by using the head only, one arm only, or one foot. Experiment with different single parts of the body for a while, and then start layering on until you are finally engaging the entire body in a whole range of movement, vacillating between subtle gesturing to movement approximating dance that incorporates the entire body.

Word's Worth

Working with a partner, attempt to achieve some predetermined objective by utilizing only words that meet some preordained, specific criterion. For example, use only words that begin with a certain phoneme or words that are three syllables in length. You might also choose to use words within a specific category, such as food items only. Your objectives should be simple, tangible ones, such as closing a door or writing one's name on the chalkboard. Try not to utilize words that directly convey the desired goal.

Do It Beautifully

As a group, devise a physical system of communication based on what the group perceives as elegant movement or gesture. Come up with about five to eight gestures and/or larger movements that the entire group can learn. These movements or gestures could include such *physicalizations* as a bow devised by the group, an elegant movement of the shoulders, a graceful turn or toss of the head, or a gentle gliding of the arms. Then with a partner or a small group, attempt to achieve an objective by utilizing only the prescribed physical vocabulary. Freely mix the gestures and movements in any way, utilizing them while traversing space or when stationary.

Elegant Deportment

Now, utilizing the same previously agreed-upon physical mode of communication, devise a code of verbal communication to integrate with the physical. That is, using the English language, use only words or types of words that the group deems to be elegant. A criterion that all words must be at least four syllables in length might serve. Another criterion might be to employ only words that are in the adverbial form using a suffix of -*ly*. Or, a category for this language might be chosen, such as relying solely on words associated with music. Attempt to achieve yet another objective utilizing both the physical and verbal vocabularies.

What's in a Name?

Choose a character's name from the following list and define an objective based on this name. For example, if playing Ranger, a simple objective to pursue is to extract a promise of an assignation with a woman in the group. If playing Lady Froth, you might seek to impress all with your endless supply of somewhat meaningless commentaries and observations on all things fashionable. As a group, move about the room as if attending a social function, and seek to achieve your objective. The group may decide to use only the group-defined physical behaviors and sounds or language, or it may choose to improvise freely.

Character Names

Sir Novelty Fashion	Worthy	Sir John Friendly	Aimwell	Sullen
Fainall	Petulant	Mrs. Marwood	Pinchwife	Sparkish
Lady Wishfort	Horner	Mrs. Dainty Fidget	Mr. Medley	Plausible
Sir Fopling Flutter	Dapperwit	Mrs. Squeamish	Sir Simon Addleplot	

FLAUNTING AS AN OBJECTIVE

A major component of behavior in Restoration society, and thus one that is reflected, celebrated, and ridiculed in the comedies, is the penchant for flaunting or displaying one's fine manners and clothing. This is another component of acting the comedies of manners with which many a beginning modern actor will struggle. Again, it is imperative not to view the objective of trying to impress others as something phony or inauthentic, as this desire was firmly rooted in the society that the comedies reflected. Further, the idea of wearing new, expensive clothing for the sole purpose of being seen while wearing it and of parading one's manners are not behaviors as foreign today as we might at first think. Certainly society's infatuation with the Academy Awards (and a host of other popular televised award productions), as well as popular film festivals, attest to this society's desire to see the "beautiful" set, and for the "beautiful" set to be seen. Not a small amount of this infatuation lies in the emphasis on fashion, as is warranted by the many magazines and televised magazine programs that dedicate significant coverage to who wore what. On a humbler note, how many of us have worn articles of new clothing with the hopes that someone might notice? How simple it is to slide a foot forward, ever-so-slightly, so that a friend or colleague might take note of a beautiful new pair of shoes. Or how readily a new jacket inspires us to walk a bit more self-consciously as we display our finery. Today it may be more difficult to imagine trying to impress someone with our wit and vocal dexterity. However, most of us can imagine times in our lives when it was, or would be, necessary to impress others with our erudition or perhaps to make an impression by demonstrating our maturity through utilizing a well-modulated voice.

With respect to acting the comedies, one may readily assume that there is always some level of flaunting or displaying involved, whether it be on a conscious or subconscious level. A character may certainly have the conscious goal of displaying her finery while walking through

St. James Park. Additionally, a character trying to win an assignation with someone of the opposite sex must in part rely on a demonstration of facility in wit and bearing. Drawing attention to one's facility was clearly a means toward impressing the desired one. Further, for the false wit, who believes his manners and clothing far surpass those of anyone else, flaunting is a way of life. For all denizens, it is fair to say that since manners and clothing were constantly being judged as a determinant of who was truly allied with the polite set, a sense of display was necessary for survival within the privileged set.

Exercises

Strutting Your Stuff

As a group, determine a set of about five to eight movements and/or gestures that are deemed aesthetically pleasing by the group at large. These need not be dance or dancelike movements but any motion or gesture the group may agree upon. Then move about the room as a group as if you are attending an important social function. Your main objective should be to impress all other attendees with your beautiful, elegant movement and bearing. Take pride in your physical life, noticing how others admire you. If creating the character of a false wit, you may want to utilize the movements a bit too lavishly and elaborate on them, making them more ornamental than originally intended.

A Fashion Statement

Continue with the previous exercise, but layer in the following: Choose one article of the clothing you are wearing and endow it with all the characteristics of the most elegant, most expensive article of clothing you can imagine. As you move about the social function, seek to impress others by flaunting this item, both subtly and not so subtly. Again, when creating a false wit, you may want to work on not-so-subtle flaunting or try selecting several articles of clothing to display.

Melodious Encounters

Continue in the group mode suggested earlier or work with a partner while attempting to impress with, and indeed flaunt, your vocal virtuosity. An interesting way in which to do this is to communicate through song, using any bit of melody or an entire piece to communicate your facility. Here too, notice how others admire your voice, and relish the experience. You may also flaunt vocal dexterity through beautifully entoned poetry of any sort as an alternative to singing.

The Joker

One way in which to experience the display of erudition or wit is to tell a joke to the group at large. Take your time and really relish the language and all the sounds of the words. Seek to impress all with your brilliance. The false wit may choose an unusually long joke or may enjoy his own humor more than his audience does.

MASKING EMOTION

As noted earlier, any heartfelt display of emotion by the leisured set was frowned upon. Likewise, the plays reflected this sensibility and did not concern themselves with any deep psychological probing on the part of the characters. This is not to say that people in the seventeenth century did not experience deep emotions nor concern themselves with their own inner psychological experiences. Rather, it was not considered socially acceptable to share these deep emotions or psychological probings with others. This is not really a difficult concept for modern actors. How many times in our lives have we found it necessary to conceal our true feelings from others? How many times have we found ourselves in social situations in which we had to don a polite mask while experiencing some sort of emotional upheaval? If young actors have not experienced much of this social masking as of yet, such situations are quite simple to imagine. For example, one can readily imagine the following scenario: You are attending a cast party that is focused on celebrating the success your friend has achieved in creating the major role of a production. However, although you thoroughly believed yourself to be more appropriate for the role with respect to experience and talent, you were not even cast in the production. Not wanting to spoil your friend's celebration, you are required to put on a celebratory mask in spite of the hurt and anger you are really experiencing.

Exercises

Hiding the Pain

A simple way in which to experiment with hiding one's true emotional state is to use the situation delineated in the previous paragraph. This can be done either as a group or in pairs. If performed with the group at large, about one-quarter of the group should be designated as those people who are feeling hurt and angry, while the other three-quarters are truly celebrating. It might be helpful to choose one person who is playing the lead role in the production. As the party is in progress, the disgruntled actors should move about the room, attempting to hide their true emotions through humor. Tell jokes, make puns, or just attempt anything you may consider to be witty to mask your feelings. If working in pairs, one person should be the leading actor and the other the disgruntled one, who tries to convince her friend that she is having a good time by using humor as a mask. Other scenarios may be created in which participants might be forced into hiding their true emotions.

Fighting Beautifully

To continue this idea of cloaking heartfelt emotion, arguing provides a perfect opportunity to mask anger or feelings of outrage. Again, this is not to say that the privileged set and the characters in the comedies did not argue. The socially prescribed manner in which to do this, however, was to do it as pleasantly or beautifully as possible. To practice this, with a partner, decide on some mutually acceptable topic on which you will disagree and then over which you will argue. At this point, it is helpful to combine the vocal and the physical aspects of cloaking, as the voice will naturally follow the physical lead and vice versa. That is, if the body is utilizing only smooth, graceful motions, the voice will likewise engage in smooth and pleasing tones. The exercise may be performed either sitting or standing. After agreeing on the topic, commence arguing, allowing yourself to utilize only elegant, graceful posture and movement. Further, the voice must be as smooth and melodic as is possible; all impulses to yell or lash out must be stifled. Fight to win the argument, all the while knowing that you can win only by employing elegant use of the body and the voice.

Poetic License

Perform basically the same exercise just described; however, this time utilize only poetic language to win the argument. Still pursue the same objective of winning the argument, which evolves out of some mutually agreed-upon topic, but use only the language of poetry from the following list (Shakespearean sonnets) or from other poetry you have memorized. Do not change the situation or the intent, only the language. Use a portion of the passage or the entire passage to communicate at any given time. Vacillate between hearing each other out and interrupting each other, as occurs in any real argument.

> Shall I compare thee to a summer's day?
>> Thou art more lovely and more temperate.
>> Rough winds do shake the darling buds of May,
>> And summer's lease hath all too short a date.
>> (Shakespeare's Sonnet 18)
>
> When I consider everything that grows
>> Holds in perfection but a little moment,
>> That this huge stage presenteth nought but shows
>> Whereupon the stars in secret influence comment . . .
>> (Sonnet 15)

Full many a glorious morning have I seen
  Flatter the mountain tops with sovereign eye,
  Kissing with golden face the meadow green,
  Gilding pale streams with heavenly alchemy . . .
  (Sonnet 33)

When most I wink, then do mine eyes best see,
  For all the day they view things unrespected;
  But when I sleep, in dreams they look on thee
  And darkly bright, are bright in dark directed.
  (Sonnet 43)

O thou, my lovely boy, who in thy power
  Dost hold Time's fickle glass, his sickle hour;
  Who hast by waning grown, and therein show'st
  Thy lovers withering as thy sweet self grow'st . . .
  (Sonnet 126)

INTERACTION AS A GAME TO BE WON

As a prelude to embracing the texts of the comedies, which rely heavily on verbal dexterity and battling with language, the following exercises will provide the actor with a feel for the use of language as a weapon or as the means to win a complex game of wit. In contemporary times, we seem not to have a corollary to this affinity for the studied use of language in day-to-day conversation. Many argue that the colloquial use of contemporary English has become very diluted and that most English speakers use a very limited range of vocabulary. One example of playing with language can be found in rap music, even if the vocabulary is based in street jargon. However, one is hard-pressed to find other examples of wordplay or clever banter, other than perhaps the somewhat witty banter associated with social gatherings among certain segments of society in Manhattan. As this subject will be addressed more thoroughly in Chapter 3, the following exercises will function as an introduction to this concept of playing with language.

Exercises

Consonant Classic

Using only either the voiced or unvoiced consonant phonemes, engage in a battle of wits with a partner wherein each person must quickly produce one of these sounds. The sounds must be returned quickly to keep the volley in play. The person to lose the game is the one who does not come up with a phoneme quickly enough or who repeats one that has already been stated. Voiced consonants include the likes of the sounds of *d*, *zh*, *g*, *v*, and *z*. Unvoiced ones would include *t*, *sh*, *k*, *f*, and *s*. After playing with one classification, switch to the other.

Verbal Volleys 1

Moving into language, with a partner, choose a short passage from any play or poetry and memorize it. The segments of Shakespeare's sonnets quoted previously function well for this exercise. After the passage is memorized, face a partner. Each person must say only one word of the passage in sequence. The one who does not return the volley, by not coming up with the next word quickly enough, loses the game. When the entire passage is completed without a stumble, continue by repeating the passage as many times as is necessary until someone "drops the ball."

Verbal Volleys 2

Next, using either the same text learned for the previous exercise or choosing another short memorized passage, engage in basically the same game. However, this time, each competitor may say as many words as he likes. The other person must then pick up the passage where his partner left off, and so on. The game continues until someone drops the ball. This exercise can also be played by a larger group, going around in a circle. Again, repeat the passage as many times as is necessary.

SCENES FOR PRACTICE

Following are several scenes from the comedies that demonstrate some of the sensibilities of the age, as well as some of the textual and performance considerations for the actor. It is helpful if the brief explanation is read prior to reading the scenes in pairs. It is also a good exercise to memorize one or more of these scenes and then improvise with them, paying particular attention to the concerns noted for each one.

Dorimant and Harriet, from Sir George Etherege's *Man of Mode*

In this scene, note how the love battle is waged through wit. Pay particular notice to the equating of love with illness and to how this metaphor is expanded by the characters until it is equated with death. Don't miss the double entendre in this comparison, particularly when the protestation of love is considered "fatal." Notice how Harriet, though infatuated with Dorimant, keeps him at bay through this battle of wits. Even Dorimant in his protestations must rely on verbal dexterity rather than an outpouring of emotion.

DORIMANT: Think of making a party, madam; love will engage.

HARRIET: You make me start! I did not think to have heard of love from you.

DORIMANT: I never knew what 'twas to have a settled ague yet, but now and then I have irregular fits.

HARRIET: Take heed! Sickness after long health is commonly more violent and dangerous.

DORIMANT: . . . Is the name of love as frightful that you dare not state it!

HARRIET: 'Twill do little execution out of your mouth on me, I am sure.

DORIMANT: It has been fatal—

HARRIET: To some easy women, but we are not all born to one destiny. I was informed you used to laugh at Love, and not make it.

Witwoud and Petulant, from William Congreve's *Way of the World*

In the following scene, the two false wits attempt to engage in witty repartee. That is, they attempt to flaunt their verbal dexterity to other characters. They are quite adept at keeping the ball in play, but their comments become insipid, even ludicrous.

WITWOUD: Raillery, raillery, Madam; we have no animosity—we hit off a little wit now and then, but no animosity. The falling out of wits is like the falling out of lovers. We agree in the main, like treble and bass. Ha, Petulant?

PETULANT: Ay, in the main. But when I have a humour to contradict—

WITWOUD: Ay, when he has a humour to contradict, then I contradict too. What, I know my cue. Then we contradict one another like two battledores, for contradictions beget one another like Jews.

PETULANT: If he says black's black—if I have a humour to say 'tis blue—let that pass—all's one for that. If I have a humour to prove it, it must be granted.

WITWOUD: Not positively must—but it may—it may.

PETULANT: Yes, it positively must, upon proof positive.

WITWOUD: Ay, upon proof positive it must; but upon proof presumptive it only may. That's a logical distinction now, Madam . . .

PETULANT: Importance is one thing, and learning's another; but a debate's a debate, that I assert.

WITWOUD: Petulant's an enemy to learning; he relies altogether on his parts.

PETULANT: No, I'm no enemy to learning; it hurts not me . . . No, no, it's no enemy to anybody but them that have it.

Mirabell and Millamant, from William Congreve's *Way of the World*

Congreve creates two of the quintessential players in the game of love in his masterpiece *Way of the World*. Although they are very nearly wed, Mirabell and Millamant continue their regular arguments, which are cloaked in some of the most masterfully comedic language of the era.

MIRABELL: Like Daphne she as lovely and as coy. Do you lock yourself up from me, to make my search more Curious? Or is this pretty Artifice contriv'd, to Signifie that here the Chase must end, and my pursuit be Crown'ed, for you can fly no further.

MILLAMANT: Vanity! No. I'll fly and be follow'd to the last moment, tho' I am upon the very Verge of Matrimony, I expect you shou'd solicite me as much as if I were wavering at the grate of a Monastery, with one foot over the threshold. I'll be solicited to the very last, nay and afterwards.

MIRABELL: What, after the last?

MILLAMANT: O, I should think I was poor and had nothing to bestow, if I were reduc'd to Inglorious ease; and free'd from the Agreeable fatigues of solicitation.

MIRABELL: But do not you know, that when favours are conferr'd upon Instant and Tedious Sollicitation, that they diminish in their value, and that both the giver Loses the grace, and the receiver lessens his Pleasure?

MILLAMANT: It may be in things of common Applicaton; but never sure in Love.

Lydia and Lady Flippant, from William Wycherley's *Love in a Wood*

In this scene, two ladies discuss the need to hide their true feelings from their lovers. Lydia reflects polite society's desire to mask affection and to deny the heartfelt emotion of love altogether. Flippant goes further by relating that even to love is a "mean" thing. Pay attention to their clever retorts to each other.

LYDIA: 'Tis as hard for a woman to conceal her indignation from her apostate lover, as to conceal her Love from her faithful servant.

LADY FLIPPANT: Or almost as hard as it is, for the prating fellows now adays, to conceal the favours of obliging Ladies.

LYDIA: If Ranger shou'd come up, (I saw him just now in the street) the discovery of my anger to him now, wou'd be as mean as the discovery of my love to him before.

LADY FLIPPANT: Though I did so mean a thing, as to love a fellow, I wou'd not do so mean a thing as to confess it, certainly, by my trouble to part with him; If I confest Love, it should be before he left me.

LYDIA: So you wou'd deserve to be left, before you were; but cou'd you ever do so mean a thing, as to confess love to any?

LADY FLIPPANT: Yes; but I never did so mean a thing, as really to love any.

LYDIA: You had once a Husband.

LADY FLIPPANT: Fye, Madam, do you think me so ill bred, as to love a Husband.

SCENE ANALYSIS

Following is an analysis of a scene from one of the most famous of the Restoration comedies of manners, William Congreve's *Way of the World*. At this point, some of the considerations highlighted in this chapter will be noted as an introduction to imagining the scene in performance. This same scene will be analyzed at the end of each subsequent chapter, so that the skills and devices analyzed within each chapter may be clearly related to scene work and performance.

Mirabell, Witwoud, Millamant, Mrs. Fainall, and Mincing from Congreve's *Way of the World*

MIRABELL: You seem to be unattended, Madam—You us'd to have the Beau-mond Throng after you; and a Flock of gay fine Perrukes hovering round you.
[*As Mirabell walks in St. James Park with Mrs. Fainall, he greets his love— Millamant—who is accompanied by three other characters. He displays his wit to all and masks his true feelings through a witty "barb." Note also that Mirabell refers to Millamant's penchant for being seen with a whole throng of fashionable people when walking in public.*]

WITWOUD: Like Moths about a Candle—I had like to have lost my Comparison for want of breath.
[*The false wit must immediately display his dexterity by interrupting an exchange that should occur between two lovers.*]

MILLAMANT: O I have deny'd my self Airs to Day. I have walk'd as fast through the Crowd—
[*Millamant, also bent on not demonstrating any warm feelings toward her lover in public, immediately commences to demonstrate her agility in this witty game.*]

WITWOUD: As a Favourite in disgrace; and with as few Followers.
[Not to miss another opportunity to flaunt his wit, Witwoud jumps back into the game, interrupting with yet another witty retort.]

MILLAMANT: Dear Mr. Witwoud, truce with your Similitudes; For I am as sick of 'em—
[Millimant gracefully tries to cut off Witwoud by again attempting to display her skill.]

WITWOUD: As a Phisician of a good air—I cannot help it Madam, tho' 'tis against myself.
[Demonstrating the false wit's proclivity for excess, Witwoud does not control himself and inserts yet another witty conclusion to Millamant's line.]

MILLAMANT: Yet again! Mincing, stand between me and his Wit.
[Millamant cleverly requests her maid to shield her from Witwoud's wit.]

WITWOUD: Do Mrs. Mincing, like a Skreen before a great Fire. I confess I do blaze to Day, I am too bright.
[Witwoud still cannot control himself and continues to demonstrate the fop's need to go too far.]

MRS. FAINALL: But dear Millamant, why were you so long?
[Interestingly, Mrs. Fainall does not wish to be a part of this game of wit.]

MILLAMANT: Long! Lord, have I not made violent haste? I have ask'd every living thing I met for you; I have enquir'd after you, as after a new Fashion.
[Millamant may well be offended by Mrs. Fainall's blunt questioning, but masks her true sentiments by flaunting her own keen dexterity in this game.]

WITWOUD: Madam, truce with your Similitudes—No, you met her Husband and did not ask him for her.
[A false wit, not aware of when he is going too far, Witwoud echoes Millamant's own words and contradicts her outright.]

MILLAMANT: By your leave Witwoud, that were like enquiring after an old Fashion, to ask a Husband for his Wife.
[However, Millamant, being one of the keenest of players in the battle of wits, effortlessly returns the volley with a cleverly fashioned witticism.]

WITWOUD: Hum, a hit, a hit, a palpable hit, I confess it.
[Even Witwoud must recognize Millamant's skill and admit defeat.]

MRS. FAINALL: You were dress'd before I came abroad.
[Mrs. Fainall is determined not to play the game and is trying to corner Millamant.]

MILLAMANT: Ay, that's true—O but then I had—Mincing what had I? Why was I so long?

[Notice Millamant's determination not to stoop to true sentiment by seeking another way out of answering Mrs. Fainall's accusations.]

MINCING: O Mem, your Laship staid to peruse a Pecquet of Letters.
[A true good servant, she has no trouble fabricating a "cover" for her mistress.]

MILLAMANT: O ay, Letters—I had Letters—I am persecuted with Letters—I hate Letters—No Body knows how to write Letters; and yet one has 'em, one does not know why—They serve one to pin up one's Hair.
[Ever-so-charmingly, Millamant skillfully masks by expanding on Mincing's fabrication.]

WITWOUD: Is that the way? Pray Madam, do you pin up your Hair with all your Letters? I find I must keep Copies.
[Witwoud again interrupts the exchange in progress, but also unwittingly assists Millamant in continuing in the masking of any true sentiment.]

MILLAMANT: Only with those in Verse, Mr. Witwoud. I never pin up my Hair with Prose. I fancy ones Hair wou'd not curl if it were pinn'd up with Prose. I think I try'd once Mincing.
[Millamant relishes this moment to flaunt her dexterity in turning the simplest observation into a cleverly ambiguous response.]

MINCING: O Mem, I shall never forget it.

MILLAMANT: Ay, poor Mincing tift and tift all morning.
[Millamant enjoys the witty diversion so much that she encourages a continuance.]

MINCING: 'Till I had the Cremp in my Fingers I'll vow Mem. And all to no purpose. But when you Laship pins it up with Poetry, it sits so pleasant the next Day as any Thing, and is so pure and crips.

WITWOUD: Indeed, so crips?
[Witwoud draws attention to Mincing's uneducated speech, most likely hoping to expand this moment around himself.]

MINCING: You're such a Critick, Mr. Witwoud.

MILLAMANT: Mirabell, Did not you take Exceptions last Night?— O ay, and went away—Now I think on't I'm angry—No now I think on't I'm pleased—For I believe I gave you some Pain.
[Millamant, determined to stay at the center of the conversation, finally decides that she has ignored her lover long enough and confronts him, cleverly denying her affection for him.]

MIRABELL: Do's that please you?
[Mirabell is, perhaps, somewhat taken aback, or he may be setting up his own witty retort.]

MILLAMANT: Infinitely; I love to give Pain.
[She continues to cleverly mask her feelings.]

MIRABELL: You wou'd affect a Cruelty which is not in your Nature; your true Vanity is in the power of pleasing.
[The love battle is finally in action, Mirabell skillfully challenging Millamant.]

MILLAMANT: O I ask your Pardon for that—One's Cruelty is one's Power, and when one parts with one's Cruelty, one parts with one's Power; and when one has parted with that, I fancy one's Old and Ugly.
[The ball is received and is returned.]

MIRABELL: Ay, ay, suffer your Cruelty to ruin the object of your Power, to destroy your Lover—And then how vain, how lost a thing you'll be! Nay, 'tis true: you are no longer handsome when you've lost your Lover; your Beauty dies upon the Instant; For Beauty is the Lover's Gift; 'tis he bestows your Charms—Your Glass is all a Cheat. The Ugly and the Old, whom the Looking-glass mortifies, yet after Commendation can be flatter'd by it, and discover Beauties in it: For that reflects our Praises, rather than your Face.
[Mirabell receives the ball and plays with it for a while by skillfully fashioning an extended, complex retort.]

MILLAMANT: O the Vanity of these Men! Fainall, dee hear him? If they did not commend us, we were not handsome! Now you must know they could not commend one, if one was not handsome. Beauty the Lover's Gift—Lord, what is a lover, that it can give? Why one makes Lovers as fast as one pleases, and they live as long as one pleases, and they die as soon as one pleases; And then if one pleases, one makes more.
[Millamant, equally as skilled, also receives the ball and plays with it for a while. She scores several points asserting a woman's control over her lovers.]

WITWOUD: Very pretty. Why you make no more of making of Lovers, Madam, than of making so many Card-matches.
[Witwoud again interrupts the game, but supports Millamant's scoring of a point.]

MILLAMANT: One no more owes one's Beauty to a Lover, than one's Wit to an Eccho: They can but reflect what we look and say; vain empty things if we are silent or unseen, And want a being.
[Ignoring Witwoud, Millamant scores even more points.]

MIRABELL: Yet to those two vain empty things, you owe two of the greatest Pleasures of Your Life.
[Mirabell must recapture the lead by setting up Millamant, forcing her into a question.]

MILLAMANT: How so?
[Millamant is seemingly weakening.]

MIRABELL: To your Lover you owe the pleasure of hearing your selves
prais'd; and to an Eccho the pleasures of hearing your selves talk.
[Mirabell flaunts his win of this round.]

WITWOUD: But I know a Lady that loves talking so incessantly, she
won't give an Eccho fair play; she has that everlasting Rotation of
Tongue, that an Eccho must wait till she dies, before it can catch her
last Words.
[Witwoud attempts to take the game into his own court.]

MILLAMANT: O Fiction; Fainall, let us leave these Men.
[Millamant may have lost the volley, but cleverly ends the game.]

NOTE

1. This writer is greatly indebted to the work of Robert Cohen, particularly his approach to performing style, as delineated in his wonderful *Acting Power*. In Chapter 4 of his text, he presents a thorough
and insightful discussion of and methods for approaching the performance of theatrical styles. Robert Cohen, *Acting Power* (Palo Alto,
CA: Mayfield, 1978), pp. 139–75.

3

THE LANGUAGE IN RESTORATION COMEDIES
Background, Types, Styles, and Modes of Speech

INTRODUCTION

As explained in Chapter 1, for the most part, Restoration comedies of manners were written to suit the tastes of the small aristocratic court coterie of Charles II. The plays, replete with wit, gallantry, the pursuit of pleasure, idleness, bawdiness, and cynicism, mirrored the fashionable world. They also reflected the manners and mores that defined polite behavior for the elite set. With the restoration of Charles, these manners and mores became quite complex. Joan Wildeblood notes that the rules of etiquette in the seventeenth century "attained a zenith of artificial complexity."[1] Accordingly, the language, as well as the structure and manner of speech in the comedies, clearly reveals the verbal practices of the polite world. Indeed, the writers found the models for their plays in the witty and refined conversation of fashionable society, which was honed and polished in the coffeehouses and other fashionable meeting places of the day. The turn of a phrase was as important, and indeed as necessary, as the graceful and seductive "turn of the calf." Wit was the cornerstone of all social interaction among the elite set, as is documented by the many surviving letters and diaries of the day. A letter written by the playwright George Etherege notes that "Sir Charles Sedley . . . would sometimes speak more wit at supper than was to be heard in any play."[2] In his dedication to *Marriage a la Mode*, Dryden clearly substantiates the socially reflective nature of the comedies, issuing the following compliment to the Earl of

Rochester:

> ...the best comic writers of our age, will join with me to acknowledge, that they have copied the gallantries of courts, the delicacy of expression, and the decencies of behavior from your Lordship, with more success, than if they had taken their models from the court of France.[3]

The skillful handling and display of witty speech is so prevalent that the focal point of the plays is not character development, but rather, in the Aristotelean sense, *diction*. Word choice and such artistic adornments as *similitudes*, *banter*, *epigrams*, and *verbal combat* take precedence and are at the center of Restoration comedies of manners. The plays are truly a celebration of the keen verbal dexterity enjoyed by the fashionable world of Restoration England.

PURVEYORS AND ANNIHILATORS OF WIT

In Chapter 2, it was noted that there are generally three classifications of character in the plays: the true wits (or simply, the wits), the false wits (the fops and fools who are pretenders to wit), and the witless (those who are either ignorant or incapable of wit or those who openly defy speaking in the mannered, artificial style). It follows, then, that there are three overall styles of speech: true wit, false wit, and speech devoid of any wit at all. Since the sparkling language lies at the center of the comedies, the language of the true wits and the false wits will be the focus of this chapter. However, a quick perusal of the language of the witless is warranted.

The third category, or the speech of the witless, can range from the simple and often undignified speech of those not a part of the polite circle (those who live in the country, for instance), to the straightforward, intentionally witless style of those who are openly opposed to artifice in speech. In the middle lie the characters who try to model themselves on the manners of the true wits, but who fail to do so. The utterances of the witless can be awkward and clumsy, as that of Ben, the seagoing son of Sir Sampson in Congreve's *Love for Love*. He is not only incapable of witty repartee, but his unaffected speech is generously sprinkled with seafaring lingo, certainly considered far too gauche for discourse in polite circles. Upon meeting Miss Prue, his intended, he declares:

> An we were a League asunder, I'de undertake to hold discourse with you, and 'twere not a main high Wind indeed and full in my Teeth. Look you forsooth, I am as it were, bound for the Land of Matrimony; 'tis a Voyage d'ee see that was none of my seeking, I was commanded by Father, and if you like of it, may-hap I may steer into your Harbour. How say you Mistress? The short of the thing is this, that if you like me, and I like you, we may chance to swing in a Hammock together.

Likewise, Miss Prue, also one of the witless, is an awkward country girl who lacks the capability to skillfully fashion an artful retort. Her rebuttal to Ben is equally as clumsy as his offer of marriage.

> ... and I'll speak truth, tho' one should always tell a lie to a man; and I don't care, let my father do what he will; I'm too big to be whipt, so I'll tell you plainly, I don't like you, nor love you at all, nor never will, what's more: So, there's your answer for you; and don't trouble me no more, you ugly thing.

Manly (the plain dealer of Wycherley's play of the same title) is more rebellious in that he not only openly defies the social practice of affected speech, but he also spurns most aspects of polite decorum. The play opens with Manly's castigation of the fop, Plausible, and, indeed, of all other socialites:

> Tell not me (my good Lord Plausible) of your Decorums, supercilious Forms, and slavish Ceremonies; your little Tricks, which you the spaniels of the Worlds do daily over and over, for, and to one another; not out of love or duty, but your servile fear.

Sir Simon Addleplot of Wycherley's *Love in a Wood,* a colorful coxcomb who believes he possesses all the elegance and ease of a true gentleman, falls far short of the elegant turn of a phrase:

> Oh the fidles, the fidles, I sent for them hither to oblige the women, not offend 'em; for I intend to Serenade the whole Park to night; but my Frolick is not without at intrigue, faith and troth; for I know the Fidles will call the whole Herd of vizard masks together; and then shall I discover if a stray'd Mistress of mine be not amongst 'em, whom I treated to night at the French-house; but as soon as the Jilt had eat up my meat, and drank her two bottles, she run away from me, and left me alone.

Clearly, these characters are incapable of, or openly resist, the practice of clever bantering and all the devices of this artifice-laden language mandated by the codes of polite society.

For the most part, however, the plays are concerned with and composed mainly of the speech of the true wits and the false wits. That is, language focuses on the polished and refined manner of speaking associated with the gallants and the ladies (true wit) and, conversely, the more affected and often overdone speech of the fops and fools (false wit). The true wits speak in a seemingly endless stream of light banter or repartee, creating clever and often colorful similitudes, double entendres, and epigrams with effortless ease. They indulge in playful banter among themselves at every turn; and they engage in sparkling, usually harmless, raillery. The false wits, though attempting to employ all the socially acceptable devices of speech, may go too far in striving to be witty or simply lack the necessary ease in polite conversation. That is, their wit may seem too contrived, or they may reveal the effort in creating that which should appear effortless. Although the wit of fops is often insipid, they will frequently go to great lengths to establish their reputations as keen wits. Additionally, lacking the sparkle of truly witty raillery, they sometimes offend their listeners.

The list of characters in the comedies that speak true wit is extensive, since all the gallants and ladies, as well as several servants and secondary characters, demonstrate facility in it. Listing only a few, Millamant and Mirabell, as well as Fainall and Mrs. Fainall (Congreve's *Way of the World*), Mellefont, Cynthia, and Careless (Congreve's *Double Dealer*), Courtall, Freeman, Gatty, and Ariana (Etherege's *She Would if She Could*), and Valentine, Angelica, and the servant Jeremy (Congreve's *Love for Love*) all demonstrate the ease and elegance of speech that indeed was not only the hallmark but the soul of Restoration comedy of manners. In the following scene, Cynthia and Mellefont in *The Double Dealer* engage in artful discourse concerning their forthcoming marriage, playing with and expanding on the metaphor of a game.

CYNTHIA: I'm thinking, that tho' Marriage makes Man and Wife One Flesh, it leaves 'em still Two Fools; and they become more Conspicuous by setting off One another.

MELLEFONT: That's only when Two Fools meet, and their follies are opposed.

CYNTHIA: Nay, I have known Two Wits meet, and by the opposition of their Wits, render themselves as ridiculous as Fools. 'Tis an odd Game we're going to Play at; what think you of drawing Stakes, and giving over in time?

MELLEFONT: No, hang't that's not endeavouring to Win, because it's possible we may lose; since we have Shuffled and Cutt, let's e'en turn up Trump now.

CYNTHIA: Then I find its like Cards if either of us have a good Hand, it is an Accident of Fortune.

MELLEFONT: No, Marriage is rather like a Game at Bowls, Fortune indeed makes the Match, and the Two nearest, and sometimes the Two farthest are together, but the game depends entirely upon Judgment.

CYNTHIA: Still it is a Game, and Consequently one of us must be a Loser.

MELLEFONT: Not at all; only a Friendly Tryal of Skill, and the Winnings to be shared between us.

Two gentlemen, Vincent and Ranger in *Love in a Wood*, demonstrate a bit of the art of witty, harmless—albeit somewhat cynical—raillery.

RANGER: What, not yet a-bed? Your man is laying you to sleep with Usquebaugh or Brandy, is it not so?

VINCENT: What Punk will not be troubled with you to night, therefore I am, is it not so?

RANGER: I have been turn'd out of doors indeed just now, by a woman, Vincent—

VINCENT: Yes, yes, your women are always such women.

RANGER: A Neighbour of yours, and I'm sure the finest you have.

VINCENT: Prythee do not asperse my Neighbourhood with your Acquaintance; 'twould bring a scandal upon an Alley.

RANGER: Nay, I do not know her, therefore I come to you.

VINCENT: 'Twas no wonder, she turn'd you out of doors then; and if she Had known you, 'twould have been a wonder she had let you stay.

Likewise, the list of fops and fools who are great pretenders to wit is seemingly endless. A short list of the characters' names alone demonstrates their want of true wit: Sparkish, Sir Foppling Flutter, Lord Foppington, Lord and Lady Froth, Tattle, Petulant, Dapperwit, and Scandal. Petulant and Witwoud in *The Way of the World* demonstrate their excellent want of true wit. Although Congreve's language is clever and humorous, the two characters are incapable of bantering as easily, concisely, and gallantly as the gentlemen do.

PETULANT: Look you Mrs. Millamant,—If you can love me dear Nymph—say it—and that's the Conclusion—pass on, or pass off,—that's all.

WITWOUD: Thous hast utter'd Volumes, Folio's, in less than Decimo Sexto, my Dear Lacedomonian, Sirra Petulant, thou art an Epitomizer of words.

PETULANT: Witwoud—You are an anihilator of sense.

WITWOUD: Thou art a retailer of Phrases; and dost deal in Remnants, like a Maker of Pincushions—thou art in truth (Metaphorically speaking) A speaker of short-hand.

PETULANT: Thou art (without a figure) Just one half of an Ass; and Baldwin yonder, thy half Brother is the rest—A gemini of Asses split, would make just four of you.

WITWOUD: Thou dost bite my dear Mustard-seed; kiss me for that.

PETULANT: Stand off—I'll kiss no more Males,—I have kiss'd your twin yonder in a humour of reconciliation, till he rises upon my stomack like a Radish.

CONVENTIONS OF PUBLIC AND PRIVATE DISCOURSE

In order for the actor to approach this artifice-laden language, it is necessary to understand some of the common practices and conventions in the plays that have their roots in the aesthetics and rules of social intercourse of the day. At the heart of understanding this opulent use of language is the awareness that the verbal mask is merely an extension—or another component—of the overall mask worn by all in the polite world. Since the authentic man or woman was judged by the outer man or woman, the exterior mask was everything. Clever language and sparkling repartee, in conjunction with lavish fashion and extensive use of makeup, presented opulent and somewhat dispassionate denizens of the fashionable world.

In this gay world, sincere or heartfelt displays of emotion were frowned upon. All sincerity of sentiment was either to remain unexpressed or was to be cloaked in clever language. This important social practice is mirrored throughout the comedies. In *Love for Love*, Mrs. Frail upbraids Valentine for wishing to speak sincerely of his lover, admonishing him that for a man, "I think his Passion ought to give place to his Manners." Since displays of heartfelt emotion were looked down on, sincere protestations of love were equally unfashionable. Further, a sense of feigned indifference was the mode. In Congreve's *Way of the World*, Witwoud notes, "A wit shou'd no more be sincere, than a woman constant." Since one was to feign indifference to love, it was equally important to pretend an aversion to marriage and to all the familiarities associated with it. The widow Lady Flippant in Congreve's *Love in a Wood* sums up this sentiment, admonishing her friend, "Fye, Madam, do you think me so ill bred, as to love a Husband." Millamant, in *The Way of the World*, skillfully pretends a loathing of all familiarities associated with marriage, declaring to her lover, Mirabell:

> I won't be called names after I'm Married, positively I won't be called Names ... Ay as Wife, Spouse, My dear, Joy, Jewel, Love, Sweet heart and the rest of that Nauseous Cant, in which Men and their wives are so fulsomely familiar. I shall never bear that—Good Mirabell don't let us be familiar or fond, nor kiss before folks, like my Lady Fadler and Sr. Francis: Nor go to Hide-Park together the first Sunday in a new chariot to provoke Eyes and Whispers; And

then never to be seen there together again; as if we were proud of one another the first Week, and asham'd of one another for ever After. Let us never visit together, nor go to a Play together, But let us be very strange and well bred.

In the plays, this feigned indifference and pretended aversion invariably leads to sex antagonism manifested in sparkling, witty love battles. Since any sincere protestation of feelings would surely afford the advantage to the other party, all players take great care to maintain the upper hand through wit. Additionally, every effort is made to force the other into declaring love first. Through denials and dissembling, lovers battle to maintain control. Harriet in Etherege's *Man of the Mode* displays a sophisticated battle of banter to keep Dorimant at bay.

DORIMANT: Is the name of love so frightful that you dare not state it?

HARRIET: 'Twill do little execution out of your mouth on me. I am sure.

DORIMANT: It has been fatal—

HARRIET: To some easy women, but we are not all born to one destiny. I was informed you used to laugh at Love, and not make it.

DORIMANT: The time has been, but now I must speak—

HARRIET: If it be on that Idle subject, I will put on my serious looks turn my head carelessly from you, drop my lip, let my Eyelids fall and hang half o'er my Eyes—thus—while you buzz a speech of an hour long in my ear, and I answer never a Word! Why do you not begin?

DORIMANT: That the company may take notice how passionately I made advances of Love! And how disdainfully you receive 'em.

HARRIET: When your Love's grown strong enough to make you bear laugh'd at, I'll give you leave to trouble me with it. Till then pray forbear, Sir.

In this passage, Harriet displays her skill in the art of dissembling, or concealing her true emotions under the pretense of an aversion to Dorimant. Although the ability to dissemble (to conceal the truth under false appearance) was practiced by all in many different situations, it was absolutely vital for ladies involved in the game of love.

Because of the keen reliance on wit and the necessity to dissemble, the love chase, as portrayed in the plays, is usually an intellectual endeavor rather than a physical one. The underlying sensuality is cloaked in language, as the lovers do battle with wit, not emotion. Further, when a pair is equally matched, as are Millamant and Mirabell in *The Way of the World*, their affected and sophisticated language reveals the quintessence of the comedy of manners love battle. Indeed all encounters between these two characters are based on verbal pyrotechnics.

MIRABELL: Like Daphne she as lovely and as coy. Do you lock yourself up from me, to make my search more Curious? Or is this pretty Artifice contriv'd, to Signifie that here the Chase must end, and my pursuit be Crown'ed, for you can fly no further.

MILLAMANT: Vanity! No. I'll fly and be follow'd to the last moment, tho' I am upon the very Verge of Matrimony, I expect you shou'd solicite me as much as if I were wavering at the grate of a Monastery, with one foot over the threshold. I'll be solicited to the very last, nay and afterwards.

MIRABELL: What, after the last?

MILLAMANT: O, I should think I was poor and had nothing to bestow, if I were reduc'd to Inglorious ease; and free'd from the Agreeable fatigues of solicitation.

MIRABELL: But do not you know, that when favours are conferr'd upon Instant and Tedious Sollicitation, that they diminish in their value, and that both the giver Loses the grace, and the receiver lessens his Pleasure?

MILLAMANT: It may be in things of common Application; but never sure in Love.

As previously noted, in following the king's lead, the pursuit of idle pleasures became an ultimate goal for the polite world. Court liaisons, indeed profligacy, were deemed proper, and fashionable society followed suit. Further, if profligacy was fashionable at court and among the polite set, it was certainly not found objectionable in the comedies. Plots are usually centered on love intrigues focusing on seduction, cuckoldry, or the attempt to extricate oneself from a no longer desirable love entanglement. It follows, then, that the subjects and modes of speech are at times clearly sexually suggestive and, at times, outright bawdy. In Wycherley's *Country Wife*, Horner has convinced the husbands of the town that he is impotent and, thus, moves freely among the ladies. In Act IV, Lady Fidget (who knows the truth about Horner) locks herself in his chamber, while her husband, Sir Jasper, laughs at "poor Horner," who contrives to get into the room. Horner tells Sir Jasper that he'll "get into her the back way, and so rifle her for it." Lady Fidget and the naive Sir Jasper continue the blatant sexual references.

SIR JASPER: Wife, my Lady Fidget, Wife, he is coming into you the back way.

LADY FIDGET: Let him come, and welcome, which way he will.

SIR JASPER: He'll catch you, and use you roughly, and he is too strong for you.

LADY FIDGET: Don't you trouble your self, let him if he can.

The uninhibited talk of love and sex was not confined to the men alone. Women in the polite circle had achieved significant emancipation and enjoyed expressing themselves as freely as men. Accordingly, in the plays, the women speak as openly and with as much relish as their male counterparts. Widows, in particular, are far more outspoken and explicit in their speech than the heroines. Widow Rich, in Etherege's *Love in a Tub*, is as at ease in a discussion about her previous liaisons as Sir Frederick is in handling the subject.

SIR FREDERICK: Have not your quarters been beaten up at the most sensible hours Before now?

WIDOW RICH: Yes; but it has been by one that has had a commission for what he did: I'm afraid shou'd it once become your Duty, you would soon grow weary of the Employment.

Another practice observed by the playwrights is to cloak the inherent bawdiness by using otherwise innocuous words. Usually, a character does this in order to conceal the true meaning of what she is saying from listeners other than the intended. In Wycherly's *Country Wife*, Horner attempts to convince Lady Fidget to stay with him by subtly relating that he is really not impotent. He intimates his sexual capability—indeed, prowess—through the use of the word *civil*.

LADY FIDGET: I will not stay with him, foh—

HORNER: Nay, madam, I beseech you stay, if it be but to see, I can be as civil to Ladies yet, as they wou'd desire.

LADY FIDGET: No, no, foh, you cannot be civil to Ladies.

In the same play, the famous "china scene" demonstrates the clever employment of the word *china* to cloak a clearly sexual connotation.

LADY FIDGET: And I have been toyling and moyling, for the pretti'st piece of China, my Dear.

HORNER: Nay she has been too hard for me do what I cou'd.

MRS. SQUEAMISH: Oh Lord I'le have some China too, too Mr. Horner, don't think to Give other people china, and me none, come in with me too.

HORNER: Upon my honour I have none left now.

MRS. SQUEAMISH: Nay, nay I have known you deny your china before now, but you Shan't put me off so, come—

HORNER: This Lady had the last there.

LADY FIDGET: Yes indeed Madam, to my certain knowledge he has no more left.

MRS. SQUEAMISH: O but it may be he may have some you could not find.

LADY FIDGET: What d'y think if he had had any left, I would not have had it too, For we women of quality never think we have China enough.

The comedies, as we have seen, are clearly mirrors of life in the Restoration court and its surrounding circle. The well-known profligacy of the court, the corresponding free, open, and sexually suggestive speech employed by both men and women, and the utter relish of witty and artful conversation are all thoroughly documented and celebrated in the Restoration comedies of manners. Yet, it can also be gleaned that the plays support yet another relished practice of the polite world—that of gossiping, a significant component of which was the making and breaking of reputations. A preponderance of the plays possess characters who seem to exist solely for this purpose. In *Love for Love*, for instance, the love of gossip is demonstrated by the names of such characters as Scandal and Tattle.

The gossip, which was sometimes gentle, but not always good-natured, covered such topics as supposed liaisons, cuckoldry, and the reputations and affectations of others. Further, no one seemingly escapes being the topic of gossip. One's friends are as likely candidates as one's enemies. Women and men alike engaged in this entertaining pastime, and the practice was not exclusive to the fops and fools. Even the heroes and heroines indulge in the lively pleasure. In *The Plain Dealer*, Olivia so masterfully demonstrates the art of gossip, she finishes others' sentences, offering her indictments of everyone named.

NOVEL: Then there's my Lady Frances, what d'ye call'er? As ugly—

OLIVIA: As a Citizens lawfully begotten daughter...

NOVEL: And there's my Lady Betty you know—

OLIVIA: As sluttish and slatternly, as an Irish woman bred in France...

PLAUSIBLE: But you can say nothing sure against the Superfine Mistress—

OLIVIA: I know who you mean. She is as censorious and detracting a Jade, as a superannuated Sinner.

DEVICES AND COMPONENTS OF WIT

Wit, which is at the heart of all Restoration comedies of manners, is nothing more than "thoughts and words elegantly adapted to the subject," according to Dryden.[4] But for contemporary actors, the language employed may seem insincere or at least far removed from today's more straightforward speech, which is almost devoid of artifice. Thus, the language is often the major stumbling block for the contemporary actor approaching these plays. For innumerable reasons, we are not the listening society that seventeenth-century England was. We may encounter a little lively banter of the style associated with New York City, or we may toss off a clever quip here and there. Clever sarcasm has become more and more in vogue since the 1980s, and we may even indulge now and then in wordplay or puns. However, very few of us speak in witty epigrams or lavish our everyday encounters with similitudes. Clearly, the clever use of language is not the sport it was in the time of Charles II. Thus, since the use of language to create wit is at the core of these comedies, it is necessary to look at the particular devices employed in order to demystify the artifice and ultimately make the language performable.

Most often, we hear the term *witty repartee* associated with this genre. It is a somewhat general term that encompasses much of the speech in the plays. Repartee is quite simply quick back-and-forth exchanges in spoken communication; the term can be used interchangeably with *banter*. Practically all characters in the comedies engage in repartee. Some are quite witty, some strive too hard to this end, and fewer (the witless) are incapable of witty repartee altogether. However, the hallmark of banter is that it is quick and lively, and the speaker seems not to pause to formulate new thoughts. It can be likened to a quick tennis match wherein the players skillfully and effortlessly maintain a volley, never dropping the ball. Most of the two-character examples used previously are excellent examples of repartee. Although bantering with the same sex could be an enjoyable pastime, the gallants and the ladies must be keen players in this game when bantering with the opposite sex. In Dryden's *An Evening's Love*, Wildblood and Jacinta display keen dexterity in repartee and reveal that they are artful players in the game. When Jacinta challenges Wildblood's professed love for her, the two expand on the image of a caged bird and engage in a beautifully witty volley.

JACINTA: What have you laid an ambush for me?

WILDBLOOD: Only to make a reprisal of my Heart.

JACINTA: 'Tis so wild, that the Lady who has it in her keeping, would be glad she were well rid on't: it does so flutter about the Cage. 'Tis a meer Bajazet; and if it be not let out the sooner, will beat out the brains against the Grates.

WILDBLOOD: I am afraid the Lady has not fed it, and 'tis wild for hunger.

JACINTA: Or perhaps it wants company; shall she put another to it?

WILDBLOOD: Ay; but then 'twere best to trust 'em out of the Cage together; let Em hop about at libertie.

JACINTA: But if they should lose one another in the wide world!

WILDBLOOD: They'll meet at night I warrant 'em.

JACINTA: But is not your heart of the nature of those Birds that breed in one Countrie, and goes to winter in another?

WILDBLOOD: Suppose it does so; yet I take my Mate along with me.

Typically, when the false wits attempt to engage in repartee, they may not be capable of coming up with new thoughts quickly enough; they may be more offensive than innocuous; they simply may lack the cleverness of the gallants and the ladies; or they may go too far, unaware that their tedious banter has become annoying to others. Petulant and Witwoud, known to be mutually contradictive, not only lack the sparkling cleverness of thought possessed by the gallants but also lack the wherewithal to control their outbursts. When questioned by Millamant as to whether they have reconciled their argument, they respond:

WITWOUD: Raillery, Raillery, madam, we have no Animosity—We hit off a little Wit now and then, but no Animosity—the falling out of Wits is like the falling out of Lovers—We agree in the main, like Treble and Bass. Ha, Petulant!

PETULANT: Ay in the main—But when I have a Humour to contradict—

WITWOUD: Ay, when he has a Humour to contradict, then I contradict too. What, I know my cue. Then we contradict one another like two Battledores, For Contradictions beget one another like Jews.

PETULANT: If he says Black's Black—If I have a Humour to say 'tis blue—Let that pass—All's one for that. If I have Humour to prove it, it must be granted.

WITWOUD: Not positively must—But it may—It may.

PETULANT: Yes, it positively must, upon Proof positive.

WITWOUD: Ay, upon Proof positive it must; but upon Proof presumptive it only may. That's a Logical Distinction now, Madam.

Raillery, an entertaining pastime practiced by the fashionable set, is equally as common a practice in the plays as repartee. Although the terms are often used interchangeably, raillery differs from repartee in that though it too relies on cleverness, it implies a sense of ridicule. The speakers are deriding or mocking another person, a group of people, or any idea or topic of conversation. It is typical to find women railing against men, and men against women. In *The Country Wife,* three ladies rail against men (and against women a bit too).

LADY FIDGET: Foh, 'tis a nasty world!

MRS. SQUEAMISH: That Men of parts, great acquaintance, and quality shou'd take up with, and spend themselves and fortunes, in keeping little Play-house Creatures, Foh.

LADY FIDGET: Nay, that Women of understanding, great acquaintance, and good quality shou'd fall a keeping too of little Creatures, foh.

MRS. SQUEAMISH: Why, 'tis the Men of qualities fault, they never visit Women of honour, and reputation, as they us'd to do; and have not so much as common civility, for Ladies of our rank, but use us with the same indifferency, and ill breeding, as if we were all marry'd to 'em.

LADY FIDGET: She says true, 'tis an errant shame Women of quality shou'd be so slighted; methinks, birth, birth, shou'd go for something; I have known Men admired, courted, and followed for their titles only.

MRS. SQUEAMISH: Ay, one wou'd think Men of honour shou'd not love no more, than marry out of their own rank.

DAINTY FIDGET: Fye, fye upon 'em, they are come to think cross breeding for themselves best as well as for their Dogs, and Horses.

LADY FIDGET: They are Dogs, and Horses for't.

MRS. SQUEAMISH: One wou'd think if not for love, for vanity a little.

DAINTY FIDGET: Nay, they do satisfy their vanity upon us sometimes; and are kind to us in Their report, tell all the world they lye with us.

LADY FIDGET: Damn'd Rascals, that we shou'd be only wrong'd by 'em; to report a Man has had a person, when he has not had a Person, is the greatest wrong in the whole World, that can be done to a person.

When used by the gallants, the ladies, and other true wits, raillery is usually good-natured and graceful, or playful with a sense of teasing. Even when the raillery of the wits is somewhat more hard-hitting and personal, the receiver rarely takes offense. Eliza, in *The Plain Dealer*, substantiates this:

> Well, but Railing now is so common, that 'tis no more Malice, but the fashion; and the absent think they are no more the worse for being rail'd at, than, the present think they are the better for being flatter'd . . .

The art of raillery is not confined to the gentlefolk, however. In *Love for Love*, Valentine's servant, Jeremy, is quite accomplished in the art, as he demonstrates by railing against wit, poetry, his master's inclination to turn poet, and, in this case, coffeehouses.

> You're undone, Sir; you're ruin'ed; you won't have a Friend left in the World, if you turn Poet—Ah Pox confound that Will's Coffee-House, it has ruin'ed more Young Men than the Royal Oak Lotter—Nothing thrives that belongs to't. The Man of the House would have been an Alderman by this time with half the Trade, if he had set up in the city—For my part, I never sit at the Door, that I don't get double the Stomach that I do at a Horse-Race. The Air upon Banstead-Downs is nothing to it for a whetter; yet I never see it, but the Spirit of Famine appears to me; sometimes like a decay'd Porter, worn out with pimping, and carrying Billet-doux and Songs; not like other Porters for Hire, but for the Jests sake. Now like a thin chairman, melted down to half his Proportion, with carrying a Poet upon Tick, to visit some great Fortune; and his Fare to be paid him like the Wages of Sin, either at the Day of Marriage, or the Day of Death.

One of the most difficult devices for contemporary actors to come to terms with is speaking in *epigrams*, or pithy sayings. The repartee of the characters is often lavishly saturated with these usually concise, pointed statements or aphorisms. They can take the form of some kind of important maxim the speaker holds to be true, or more typically, they may be utilized simply to strengthen any contention whatsoever. In this day and age, it is rare to find people who liberally lace their speech with epigrams. Thus, people like Ross Perot are generally held to be colorful, eccentric, if not old-fashioned, speakers. In the comedies, epigrams are used by the characters to sum up their beliefs or sentiments on any subject, ranging from gambling and the opposite sex to the world at large. At the very beginning of *The Way of the World*, Fainall tells Mirabell that he is playing cards "too negligently," and that he (Fainall) will not play on because "the coldness of a losing Gamester lessens the Pleasure of the winner." Further, he would "no more play with a Man that slighted his ill Fortune, than [he'd] make Love to a Woman who undervalu'd the Loss of her Reputation." Lady Flippant, in *Love in a Wood*, rails to Ranger that men are untrustworthy and drives her point home with "Quacks in their Bills, and Poets in the titles of their Plays, do not more disappoint us, than Gallants with their promises; but I trust none." And in *The Plain*

Dealer, Eliza admonishes Olivia, who bemoans that she is weary of the world, "the World is but a constant Keeping Gallant, whom we fail not to quarrel with, when any thing crosses us, yet cannot part with't for our hearts." Even many of the servants are quite adept at creating witty and meaningful epigrams. Lucy, in *The Country Wife*, admonishes Alithea, who is insistent on marrying the coxcomb Mr. Sparkish even though she is in love with Mr. Harcourt. Alithea believes she will begin to love Sparkish after marriage. Lucy tells her:

> The Woman that marries to love better, will be as much mistaken, as the Wencher that marries to live better. No, Madam, marrying to encrease love, is like gaming to become rich; alas you only loose what little stock you had before.

One of the primary means of demonstrating facile wit is through the use of *similitudes*, or what we would call *similes* today. A figure of speech by which one thing is likened to another, similitudes are employed to a great extent by the true wits and false wits alike. The true wits tend to be more economic in the creation of similitudes than are the fops. In *Love in a Wood*, the two gallants Vincent and Ranger trade a few brief but well-pointed ones.

RANGER: Incredulous envy; thou art as envious, as an impotent Letcher at a Wedding.

VINCENT: Thou are either mad, or as vain as a French-man, newly return'd home from a Campaign, or obliging England.

RANGER: Thou art as envious as a Rival.

The gallant Wildblood, in Dryden's *An Evening's Love*, creates a very clever and more developed similitude comparing men to cats: "we love to get our Mistresses and purr over 'em, as Cats do over Mice, and then let 'em go a little way: and all the pleasure is to pat 'em back again."

It is the fops and fools, however, who relish the frequent and lavish use of similitudes, often to the chagrin of their listeners. Frequently, the fops seemingly cannot control themselves and must create one similitude after another in order to prove the enormity of their wit. In *Love in a Wood*, Martha agrees to marry the fop Dapperwit. The marriage must be accomplished in great haste before Martha's father discovers their plans. However, Dapperwit cannot budge until he has created an apt similitude for "wit without vanity," almost losing Martha in the process. As she attempts to leave, he stops her with:

> Are you so impatient to be my Wife? He is like—he is like—a Picture without shadows, or, or—a Face without Patches—or a Diamond without a Foyl; these are new thoughts now, these are new.

Earlier in the same play, Dapperwit demonstrates the same obsession with similitudes when Ranger asks Dapperwit's help in hurrying to arrange a liaison between Christina and himself. Again, rather than make haste, Dapperwit would feign develop one similitude after another, requiring Ranger to stop him in his reverie. So enamored is he with his own similitudes, his first one is twice removed from its subject—himself.

DAPPERWIT: I take as much pleasure to bring Lovers together, as an old Woman, that as a Bankrupt Gamester loves to look on, though he has no advantage by the Play; or as a Bully that fights not himself, yet takes pleasure to set people together by the ears; or as—

RANGER: S'death, is this a time for similitudes?

Witwoud, in *The Way of the World,* has the same penchant for the creation of similitude after similitude. Even when Millamant, after suffering through several, requests an end to similitude making, Witwoud cannot control himself.

MILLAMANT: Dear Mr. Witwoud, truce with your Similitudes; For I am as sick of 'em—

WITWOUD: As a Phisician of a good Air—I cannot help it Madam, tho' 'tis against Myself.

MILLAMANT: Yet again! Mincing, stand between me and his Wit.

WITWOUD: Do Mrs. Mincing, like a Skreen before a great Fire. I confess I do blaze to Day, I am too bright.

Another delightful practice engaged in is the use of double entendres, or cleverly using words or phrases with more than one meaning, one of which may be sexually suggestive. Both wits and false wits alike indulge in these, not only to flaunt their facility but also merely for their own enjoyment. Typically, however, double entendres are used to signal a private meaning to another (most often a potential lover) and are usually created at the expense of someone else (frequently, the potential lover's spouse). In *The Double Dealer,* Lord Froth foolishly allows his wife, Lady Froth, great liberty with the coxcomb Brisk. In encouraging his Lady to show Brisk some samples of her writing, he asks, "Have you nothing about you to shew him, my Dear?" To which she responds, "Yes, I believe I have.—Mr. Brisk, come will you go into the next Room? And there I'll shew you all I have." Later in the same play, Lord Froth is the hapless victim of double entendres when Sir Paul not-so-subtly suggests that Lady Froth has been engaging in more than literary discussion with Brisk.

LORD FROTH: ... Where's my Wife?

SIR PAUL: All turn'd topsie turvey, as sure as a Gun.

LORD FROTH: How do you mean? My Wife!

SIR PAUL: The strangest posture of Affairs!

LORD FROTH: What, my Wife?

SIR PAUL: No, no, I mean the Family.—your Lady's Affairs may be in very good Posture; I saw her go into the Garden with Mr. Brisk.

LORD FROTH: How? Where, when, what to do?

SIR PAUL: I suppose they have been laying their heads together.

LORD FROTH: How?

SIR PAUL: Nay, only about Poetry, I suppose, My Lord; making Couplets.

Finally, Sir Jasper, in *The Country Wife*, unwittingly creates double entendres at his own expense when he allows his wife, Lady Fidget, to go off with Horner, the self-proclaimed eunuch. He tells her, "Get you gone to your business together; go, go, to your business, I say, pleasure, whilst I go to my pleasure, business." To which Lady Fidget composes the final rhymed couplet of the scene, cleverly picking up on Sir Jasper's own double entendre.

Who for his business, from his Wife will run;
Takes the best care, to have her bus'ness done.

Two other general terms need to be considered when evaluating the structure of the language in the comedies of manners: *rant* and *cant*. Although cant may be witty, rant is usually devoid of wit. Rant, which is interesting inasmuch as overt display of emotion was frowned upon in polite society of Restoration England, is nothing more than wild— usually angry—speech. Thus, contrary to the manners of the time, it is typically a loud display of emotion. In the plays, it is usually the old fops or fools who do not maintain decorum and stoop to ranting. Typically, many rants are ignited by a character's suspicion that he is being cuckolded or wronged in love. However, the fear of losing a daughter to a worldly gallant or of losing part or all of one's fortune can also provide the fuel for these outbursts. One of the most obvious scenarios for ranting is clearly when a lover feels she or he has been wronged, particularly in the cases of older, married lovers or spouses. Lady Touchwood finds that her supposed lover, Maskwell, is really in love with Cynthia in *The Double Dealer*. His feigned love to her Ladyship was merely a part of a larger intrigue. When Lord Touchwood leaves the scene after innocently revealing that Maskwell is in love with Cynthia, Lady Touchwood unleashes her fury.

> ... damn'd Villain! Oh, I am wild with this surprize of treachery; hell and Fire, it is impossible, it cannot be,—he love Cynthia! What have I been Bawd to his designs? His Property only, a baiting place to stay his stomach in the road to her ... Shame and Destruction! I cannot bear it, oh! What Woman can bear to be a Property? To be kindled to a flame, only to light him to anothers Arms; oh! That I were Fire indeed, that I might burn the vile Traytor to a Hell of torments,—but he's Damnation proof, a Devil already, and Fire in his Element ... all my designs are lost, my Love unsated, my Revenge unfinished, and fresh cause of fury from unthought of Plagues.

Cant, on the other hand, is quite the opposite of rant, in that it is insincere talk. It may have the mask of true emotion, but it is uttered by people who are dissembling, particularly in a declaration of love. That is, the speaker may suggest heartfelt emotion through the use of colorful language in his or her declaration, but at the core is a lie. Typical cants focus on falsely declaring love as a means to gain a one-time assignation or gulling an old fool or widow as part of some intricate love scheme to attain someone else. *The Double Dealer* provides one of the most humorous cants in the comedies. The character of Careless feigns love to Lady Plyant as a part of the same complicated love intrigue suggested earlier.

> Ah heavens, madam, you ruine me with Kindness; your Charming tongue pursues the Victory of your Eyes, while at your Feet your poor Adorer dies ... Ah why are you so Fair, so bewitching Fair? O let me grow to the ground here, and feast upon that hand; O let me press it to my heart, my aking trembling heart. The nimble movement shall instruct your Pulse, and teach to allarm Desire. (*Aside*) Zoons I'm almost at the end of my Cant, if she does not yield quickly ... And must you leave me! Rather let me Languish out a Wretched Life, and breathe my soul beneath your feet. (*Aside*) I must say the same thing over again, and can't help it.

SUMMARY

In the small coterie of Restoration court society and the polite world surrounding it, the use of witty, refined language was a cornerstone of all interaction. Thus, in Restoration comedies of manners, which reflect the manners of this world, the creation of wit is all-important. Accordingly, there are three overall types of characters (true wits, false wits, and the witless) who demonstrate the three major categories of speech: true wit, false wit, and language void of wit altogether. The rules that govern the creation of wit are rooted in the decorum and manners of Restoration contemporary society. In life, and thus in the plays, the expression of heartfelt emotion—particularly the profession of true love—was frowned upon. Lovers were expected to feign indifference and pretend an aversion to marriage. In the plays, the classic love battles are rooted in and ignited by these rules of decorum. Lovers attempt to maintain the upper hand through wit and by dissembling and denying their love, endeavoring to force their opponent to declare his or her love first. The battles are, therefore, more intellectual than sensual or physical, and they often result in a fine display of verbal pyrotechnics.

The court of Charles II was known for its bawdiness and licentiousness, and the plays mirror this sensibility with plots centering on love intrigues, seduction, and cuckoldry. Women speak as freely of sex and love as do the men. Gossip, often concerning sexual intrigues in particular, was a favorite pastime, and characters in the plays relish the game.

The wit, both in life and in the plays, is demonstrated particularly through repartee, or the quick exchange of clever thoughts, as well as raillery, which also can be very clever but implies a sense of ridicule or mocking. Other devices include the use of epigrams (pithy sayings or proclamations) and similitudes (the practice of likening one thing or idea to another nonrelated thing or idea). Double entendres are used for one's own enjoyment and often to signal a private meaning to a potential lover. They are also employed when characters create them unwittingly, often at their own expense. Finally, rant (loud emotional speech) and cant (the use of insincere verbal sentiment typically employed in an expression of feigned love) are two other common practices indulged in throughout the plays.

EXERCISES

Relishing the Words

1. Facing a partner, stand or sit comfortably. Utilizing only numbers as your vocabulary, have a scintillating conversation on a mutually agreed-upon subject, counting from one to fifty. Each person may count as many numbers as necessary, making sure each person has the opportunity to speak. As you count, discover numbers (or the sound of certain numbers) that you particularly like and that you can really relish. Gossiping works very well for this exercise, as does a discussion of one's latest tryst or lover, but use your imagination to come up with any topic. Convey the subtext through the sound of the words and the feel of the words in your mouth. You may

perform this same exercise using the alphabet or by employing only gibberish.

2. You are a nightclub singer who is absolutely in love with his voice, and the remainder of the class is the audience. Sing any song you choose (ranging from any current pop song to an operatic aria) *a capella*, and in the most heartfelt manner you can imagine, but in a style typical to nightclub singers or song "stylists." Relish certain sounds of words, certain pitches, or the way you color a certain word with your voice. Absolutely fall in love with the words of your song and the sound of your own voice.

3. Choose and memorize any of the following short passages. On your own, speak the words, allowing the sounds to live in your mouth, your head, your chest, and your whole body. Relish the sound and the feel of certain words or phrases. Then speak the text to the whole class or to a partner, sharing your relish of the words, the sound of the words, and your own voice.

HEARTWELL, FROM CONGREVE'S *OLD BATCHELOUR*

Oh Manhood, where art thou! What am I come to? A Womans Toy; at these years! Death, a bearded Baby for a Girl to dandle. O dotage, dotage! That ever that Noble passion, Lust, should ebb to this degree—No reflux of vigorous Blood; But milky Love, supplies the empty Channels; and prompts me to the softness of A Child—A meer Infant and would suck.

LOVELESS, FROM VANBRUGH'S *RELAPSE*

Can you then doubt my constancy, Amanda?
You'll find 'tis built upon a steady basis—
The rock of reason now supports my love,
On which it stands so fix'd,
The rudest hurricane of wild desire
Wou'd, like the breath of a soft slumbering babe,
Pass by, and never shake it.

AMANDA, FROM VANBRUGH'S *RELAPSE*

Yet still 'tis safer to avoid the storm
The strongest vessels, if they put to sea,
May possibly be lost.
Wou'd I cou'd keep you here in this calm port for ever!
Forgive the weakness of a woman,
I am uneasy at your going to stay so long in town;
I know its false insinuating pleasures;
I know the force of its delusions;
I know the strength of its attacks;
I know the weak defence of nature;
I know you are a man—and I—a wife.

HEARTFREE, FROM VANBRUGH'S PROVOK'D WIFE

What you have undone by art! It made you handsome; it gave you beauty to a miracle, a shape without a fault, wit enough to make them relish and so turn'd you loose to your own discretion; which has made such work with you, that you are become the pity of our sex, and the jest of your own. There is not a feature in your face, but you have found the way to teach it some affected convulsion; your feet, your hands, your very fingers ends are directed never to move without some ridiculous air or other; and your language is suitable trumpet, to draw people's eyes upon the raree-show.

LADY WISHFORT, FROM CONGREVE'S WAY OF THE WORLD

O Sir Rowland, the hours that he has dy'd away at my Feet, the Tears that he has shed, the Oaths that he has sworn, the Palpitations that he has felt, the Trances and the Tremblings, the Ardors and the Ecstacies the Kneelings and the Riseings, the Heart-heavings, and the Hand-Gripings, the Pangs and the Pathetick Regards of his protesting Eyes! Oh no memory can Register.

ASTERIA, FROM DRYDEN'S SECRET LOVE

The hardest term she for your act could find
Was onely this, O Philocles, unkind!
Then, setting free a sigh, from her fair eyes
She wip'd two pearls, the remnants of mild show'rs,
Which hung, like drops upon the bells of flowers:
And thank'd the Heav'ns,
Which better did, what she design'd, pursue,
Without her crime to give her pow'r to you.

Similitudes

1. An excellent way to achieve the feel for creating similitudes is to be forced into creating them on the spot. Do not worry; they need not be witty or even very good. It is the process of creating them and the relish of your own brilliance that you want to pay attention to. The class may stand or sit in a circle, and one person starts off by developing the first half of a similitude, such as, "My morning was so bad it was as if..." Then, the next person in the circle must finish it. After this step, the third person must repeat the entire similitude, relishing the beauty and wit of it. The process then continues on with the second person in the circle starting a similitude, the third finishing it, and the fourth repeating the entire phrase. Continue in this manner until all students have participated in all steps of the process. Other ideas could include

   "My last boyfriend was so attractive, he was like..."
   "Shelley's (the name of a student in the class) outfit is as lovely as..."
   "Studying for midterm exams is so painful, it's like..."

Again, use your own imagination to come up with ideas that will be appealing to your fellow class or cast members.

2. The following exercise is particularly helpful when playing the character of a fop or false wit. Either in pairs, or as the whole class, decide on the first half of a similitude. Then, individually, think of three or four different completions to the similitude, which are either insipid, boring, stupid, or just plain meaningless. Then go back and forth in your pair, or around the circle, or randomly interrupt each other and compete with your similitudes. Flaunt and relish your own similitudes, at the same time revealing, perhaps, how boring you find the others. Outdo the others, knocking down all that precedes your similitude. When you run out of similitudes on that topic, or simply tire of it, change to a new one.

3. In order to get a better feel for the period language, perform the same exercise as in step 2, choosing and memorizing two or three similitudes from the following list.

AMANDA, FROM VANBRUGH'S *RELAPSE*

Like a young puppy in a warren, they have a flirt at all, and catch none.

LYDIA, FROM WYCHERLEY'S *LOVE IN A WOOD*

'Tis as hard for a woman to conceal her indignation from her apostate Lover, as to conceal her Love from her faithful servant.

LYDIA, FROM *LOVE IN A WOOD*

He is like the desperate Banke-routes of this age, who if they can get people's fortunes into their hands, care not though they spend them in Goale, all their lives.

DAPPERWIT, FROM *LOVE IN A WOOD*

A Lady disappointed by her Gallant, the night before her journey, cou'd not be more touchy with her Maid, or Husband, than you are with me now, after your disappointment.

DAPPERWIT, FROM *LOVE IN A WOOD*

Wit without vanity is like . . . a Picture without Shadows . . . or a Face without Patches—or a Diamond without a Foyl.

HORNER, FROM WYCHERLEY'S *COUNTRY WIFE*

'Tis as hard to be a good Fellow, a good Friend, and a Lover of Women, as 'tis to be a good Fellow, a good Friend, and a Lover of Money.

WITWOUD, FROM CONGREVE'S *WAY OF THE WORLD*

Friendship without Freedom is as dull as Love without enjoyment, or Wine without Toasting.

WITWOUD, FROM *THE WAY OF THE WORLD*

She hates Mirabell worse than a Quaker hates a parrot, or than a Fishmonger hates a hard Frost.

4. With a partner, memorize the following short *open scene*, deciding who will play A and who, B. After memorizing the scene, first try improvising completions to the similitudes. Try this several times, until you find the ones you like best. With your partner, decide on the context of the scene (the *who*, *what*, and *where*), as well as your intention. Then rehearse the scene with your partner, again relishing the brilliance of your own similitudes and using them to score points, so to speak, in the scene. Eventually, perform the scene for the entire class.

A: I missed you last night. I was so lonely it was like . . .

B: Sorry, I was so busy with work it was as if . . .

A: Oh, I thought you said you were off last night.

B: Oops, sorry. I forgot to tell you. I swear my memory is as bad as . . .

A: Well I walked by your office and I didn't see you. I swear my eyesight is as good as . . .

B: I must have just stepped out. See you tonight?

A: I don't know. My schedule is so jammed it's like a . . .

B: Well, if you can fit me in, I'd like to see you as much as . . .

Epigrammatic Speaking

1. As a group, make a quick list of pithy sayings, such as: "A penny saved is a penny earned"; "Don't count your chickens before they're hatched"; "You can dress them up but you can't take them anywhere"; and so on. You might write these on a chalkboard or an easel so that they are readily available to all the participants. As a group, move about the room as if you are attending a swank party, using these epigrams to socialize, repeating them and choosing new ones as needed. When encountering someone (or a group of people), share your epigram as if it were the most insightful, witty, or brilliant epigram ever devised. Let interactions happen and relationships develop.

2. Do the same exercise explained in step 1, but make up your own silly epigrams. You may mix metaphors ("Don't count a penny saved until it's hatched"). They may be truly clever; they may be

utter nonsense ("One's are much like two's—you can take them anywhere, but you can't dress them up!").

3. Choose two or more of your favorite epigrams from the previous two exercises and memorize them. Now decide if you are a true wit or a false wit. In a group of three or four, decide on a topic of discussion—any topic will do—keeping in mind that such topics as someone's latest intrigue or gossip about some nonpresent person are always a good choice. Make yourselves comfortable in an intimate conversation circle. As you converse on your topic, drop in your silly epigrams wherever you believe them to fit. However, do not be concerned whether or not the appropriateness is truly meaningful. Drive a point home with them; show off your erudition; or snub others you believe to be witless. Use your imagination! If you are a true wit, they should roll off your tongue effortlessly. If you are a false wit, you might strive a little harder to create them, or you may go too far in using them too lavishly.

4. Play any version of the previous exercises utilizing any of the following epigrams from the plays.

MANLY, FROM WYCHERLY'S *PLAIN DEALER*

Thus Women, and Men like Women, are too hard for us, when they think we do not hear 'em; and Reputation, like other Mistresses, is never true to a Man in his absence.

MANLY, FROM *PLAIN DEALER*

Damn'd Money! It's Master's potent rival still; and, like a saucy Pimp, corrupts it self, the Mistress it procures for us.

MILLAMANT, FROM CONGREVE'S *WAY OF THE WORLD*

Well, 'tis a lamentable thing I'll swear, that one has not the liberty of choosing one's Acquaintance, as one does one's Cloaths.

BELLMOUR, FROM CONGREVE'S *OLD BATCHELOUR*

When Wit and Reason, both, have fail'd to move;
Kind Looks and Actions (from Success) do prove,
Ev'n Silence may be Eloquent in Love.

BELLAMY, FROM DRYDEN'S *AN EVENING'S LOVE*

We will attempt the Mistress by the Maid,
Women by women still are best betray'd.

JACINTA, FROM *AN EVENING'S LOVE*

None but fools confine their pleasure: what Usurer ever thought his coffers held too much? No, I'll give my self the swinge, and love without reserve. If I'll keep a passion, I'll never starve it in my service.

LUCY, FROM WYCHERLY'S COUNTRY WIFE

The woman that marries to love better, will be as much mistaken, as the Wencher that marries to live better. No, Madam, marrying to encrease love, is like gaming to become rich; alas you only loose, what little stock you had before.

HORNER, FROM *THE COUNTRY WIFE*

As gout in Age, from Pox in Youth proceeds;
So Wenching past, then jealousy succeeds:
The worst disease that Love and Wenching breeds.

HORNER, FROM *THE COUNTRY WIFE*

Mistresses are like Books; if you pore upon them too much, they doze you, and make you unfit for company; but if us'd discreetly, you are the fitter for conversation for them.

HORNER, FROM *THE COUNTRY WIFE*

... there are Quacks in love, as well as Physick, who get but the fewer and worse Patients, for their boasting: a good name is seldom got by giving it ones self, and Women no more than honour are compass'd by bragging.

Verbal Battles and Bantering

1. With a partner, engage in a verbal battle using a limited vocabulary. That is, decide on a category, such as colors, food, or clothing, and compete with your partner using only descriptions of objects in the selected category. Play to win by relishing your own cleverly devised descriptions, and by knocking down your partner's, striving to outdo his. Choose certain words or sounds of words to be the actual artillery with which you battle. Relish all your own victories, but stay keenly aware of the other person's. You may then add to the cleverness of your speech and increase the challenge by imposing certain rules. You may choose to speak solely in alliteration, perhaps require that each person use a set amount of words in each exchange, or do both. For example, if you are competing with clothing, the battle may go something like this:

   A: Sumptuously slinky silk shirts!

   B: Glittering gorgeous garish gowns!

   A: Terrific taupe tweed trousers!

   B: Polished pointed pink pumps!

   Remember, it is important that the volley is returned quickly. Be careful: This does not mean that one speaks fast. Rather, take your time in relishing your words. You may also take time in stretching the sounds of each word, but without pausing in between your own words and the other person's. The idea of dovetailing your lines with your partner's is important.

2. With a partner, memorize the following open scene. Choose a category, again, anything from food, to clothing, to colors, and so on. You may stick to using nouns only, or you may choose to elaborate your nouns using clever or even silly descriptions. The important component of this exercise is that although you are in profound disagreement, you are attempting to disagree with your partner in a clever, artful manner. Here, too, keep the bantering moving forward while you are waging verbal battle.

A: I truly believe that I should have the _____ .

B: Of course, you should like to have the _____ , but it is a far better thing that we have the _____ .

A: Well, if it is a "far better thing that we have the _____ ," then I certainly shall have no part of your _____ .

B: Part of my _____ ? Well I would no more share my _____ with you than I would have your _____ .

A: Fine. Then let's just make it _____ and be done with it!

B. Fine. But I think I'll make it _____ and be done with it!

3. Choose any short two-character stichomythic scene from classical to contemporary dramatic literature and memorize it. Then without any consideration of the given circumstances of the actual play or the actual meaning and subtext of the words, perform the scene as a battle of wits. Choose specific words or sounds from your lines that you particularly like and use these to win at the game. Again, let these words or sounds be the artillery. Scenes that are based on short, quick exchanges are best suited to this exercise. Many scenes from the works of Mamet, Pinter, Beckett, and Shakespeare function well. Following are two examples that function well for this exercise.

RICHARD, DUKE OF GLOUCESTER, AND LADY ANNE, FROM SHAKESPEARE'S *KING RICHARD III*

LADY ANNE: I would I knew thy heart.

RICHARD: 'Tis figured in my tongue.

LADY ANNE: I fear me both are false.

RICHARD: Then never man was true.

LADY ANNE: Well, well, put up your sword.

RICHARD: Say, then, my peace is made.

LADY ANNE: That shalt thou know hereafter.

RICHARD: But shall I live in hope?

LADY ANNE: All men, I hope, live so.

RICHARD: Vouchsafe to wear this ring.

LADY ANNE: To take is not to give.

AMANDA AND LOVELESS, FROM VANBRUGH'S RELAPSE

AMANDA: Ay, there take heed.

LOVELESS: Indeed the danger's small.

AMANDA: And yet my fears are great.

LOVELESS: Why are you so timorous?

AMANDA: Because you are so bold.

LOVELESS: My courage should disperse your apprehensions.

AMANDA: My apprehensions should alarm your courage.

LOVELESS: Fy, fy, Amanda, it is not kind thus to distrust me.

AMANDA: And yet my fears are founded on my love.

LOVELESS: Your love then is not found as it ought.

4. Choose either the Millamant and Mirabell scene or the Dorimant and Harriet scene, quoted earlier, and do the same as in step 3.

Private Vocabularies and Innocent Words

1. With a partner, decide on some category that will provide many potential innocent words and improvise a discussion on some non-related topic of keen interest. For example, a category might be *school lunches* and could include such references or loaded words as *sandwich, lunch box/bag, thermos,* and *juice box.* After improvising for approximately five minutes, the exercise opens out to the whole group, which is now attending a party or any other social gathering. As the participants move around the gathering, the group leader should point out a certain pair to engage in their planned conversation. All others should attempt to listen, without appearing to be eavesdropping. A probable conversation might go as follows:

A: I saw her yesterday with her lunchbox in hand.

B: As did I. However, she did not have her thermos.

A: Shocking! Not to mention that she conveniently forgot her juice box.

B: Well, I'm sure it was also just an oversight that she did not have her banana!

Be sure to relish being in the know, and always assume that your private vocabulary is at the expense of someone else in attendance.

2. Here too, you may utilize any short stichomythic scene from dramatic literature. Again, pay no heed to the actual circumstances and subtext. With your partner, decide on the topic at hand, and within the larger group, convey your meaning to the other person and relish your secret knowledge.

Dissembling and Feigned Indifference

1. With a partner (or within a larger group), fabricate and convey an incredible lie. For example, tell the story of some event that you supposedly experienced, elaborating more and more as the story develops. Tell the lie in your most convincing manner; do not show or "play" the lie.

2. With a partner, mutually decide on a topic upon which you can profoundly disagree. Although it may be a topic of actual disagreement, it is not necessary to the exercise that it is. You may, for instance, decide to disagree about the color of someone's hair or the proper length for a skirt or jeans. Regardless, the disagreement, real or feigned, must be profound. Then improvise an argument, in which although you profoundly disagree, you take great pains not to show your anger, frustration, or impatience. This does not mean that you do not feel these emotions, but that you cloak them in words and voice. Again, these improvised conversations need not be particularly witty, as it is the masking of emotions that is important. In fact, allow yourself to experience the tension between the authentic self and the mask created with your words.

3. Memorize one of the following short scenes. With a partner, use the words of the scene to dissemble in the way inherently suggested; that is, assume that each of the characters is lying.

RANGER AND LADY FLIPPANT, FROM WYCHERLY'S LOVE IN A WOOD

LADY FLIPPANT: Yet you must know, Sir, my aversion to marriage is such, that you nor no Man breathing, shall ever perswade me to it.

RANGER: Curs'd be the man shou'd do so rude thing as to perswade you to any Thing against your inclination; I wou'd not do it for the World, Madam.

LADY FLIPPANT: Come, come, though you seem to be a civil Gentleman, I think you no Better than your Neighbours; I do not know a man of you all, that will not thrust a Woman into a corner, and then talk an hour to her impertinently of marriage.

RANGER: You wou'd find me another man in a corner, I assure you, Madam, for you shou'd not have a word of marriage from me, whatsoever you might find in my actions of it; I hate talking as much as you.

LADY FLIPPANT: I hate it extreamly.

RANGER: I am your man then, Madam, for I find just the same fault with your Sex as you do with ours; I ne'er cou'd have to do with a Woman in my life, but still She wou'd be impertinently talking of marriage to me.

RANGER AND LYDIA, FROM *LOVE IN A WOOD*

RANGER: Indeed cousin, besides my business, another cause, I did not wait on you, was, my apprehension, you were gone to the Park, notwithstanding your promise to the contrary.

LYDIA: Therefore, you went to the Park, to visit me there, notwithstanding your promise to the contrary.

RANGER: Who, I at the Park? when I had promis'd to wait upon you at your lodging; but were you at the Park, Madam?

LYDIA: Who, I at the Park? when I had promis'd to wait for you at home; I was no more at the Park than you were; were you at the Park?

RANGER: The Park had been a dismal desart to me, notwithstanding all the good company in't; if it had wanted yours.

Raillery, Rant, and Cant

1. With a partner, or in a larger group, agree on a highly charged topic against which both (or most within the group) can rail readily. Today, we might say that we are "ragging on" something or someone. Then first, with your partner or as a group, unleash your fury or vent your frustration. This should be done in the students' own colloquial language, and turns may be taken; however, it is fine to interrupt and even speak at the same time. Next, although you may still use the same language, rail against the topic at hand, but attempt to gloss over the underlying emotion. That is, you may become aware of making your voice more pleasant or melodious,

speaking your own language more carefully and articulately, or even editing it or refining it. If possible, attempt to employ similitudes and other witticisms, even if they are not particularly witty.

2. As previously mentioned, for the most part it is the fools and fops who rant. However, this is a useful and fun exercise for all to experience. When ranting, the character is usually blustering. When improvising this sort of character, it is sometimes difficult to improvise the necessary vocabulary. To facilitate this process, as a group, write up a list of perhaps ten to twelve colorful adjectives and adverbs on a chalkboard or an easel. On your own, decide what kind of character you generally are—elderly, rich, widowed, and so forth. Only surface information is necessary. Then decide how you have been wronged. That is, you have been scorned in love, outwitted by a rival with respect to money, or gulled by your own offspring, for example. Then choose someone to whom you will direct your rant and characterize that person as either the subject of your scorn or a sympathetic listener. Then start ranting against the wrongdoer, and as you speak, glance to the board and extract colorful adjectives and adverbs to integrate into your rant, if necessary. Do not worry about stumbling in your speech or resorting to fillers. This search for the right words can be a useful tool in creating the type of character who resorts to ranting. However, be careful of breaking character or stopping to find the words. Continue at all costs and keep the energy up!

3. Choose a partner, but then on your own, decide on some aspect of your partner that you wish to praise ingenuously. You may choose his hair, clothing, eyebrows, backpack, athletic shoes, or glasses, for instance. The choice is insignificant. Although the sentiment need not be authentic for you personally, but only for your character, make the decision that you absolutely disdain the object or aspect of praise. Now improvise several sentences of glorification, of absolute adoration. Perform your cant to your partner—with the rest of the group observing—and insert an aside after each item of adulation. That is, let the audience in on your character's authentic feelings concerning the item of praise. Maintain the convention that only the audience hears and is aware of the asides. Further, be sure to maintain at all times a semblance of sincerity when addressing your partner.

4. Select from the following list one of the short rants or cants to direct to a partner. Memorize it, making quick, only cursory, character choices. Taking turns, rehearse the rant or cant, maintaining

the intensity for the rant and a sense of feigned sincerity for the cant.

Rants

PINCHWIFE, FROM WYCHERLY'S *COUNTRY WIFE*

Oh woman, damn'd woman, and Love, damn'd Love, their old Tempter, for this is one of his miracles, in a moment, he can make those blind that cou'd see, and those see that were blind, those dumb that could speak, and those prattle who were dumb before, nay what is more than all, make these dowbak'd, sensless, indocile animals, women, too hard for us their Politick Lords and Rulers in a moment.

LADY WISHFORT, FROM CONGREVE'S *WAY OF THE WORLD*

Out of my house, out of my house, thou Viper, thou Serpent, that I have foster'd thou bosome traytress, that I rais'd from nothing—begon, begon, begon, go, go,—that I took from Washing of old Gause and Weaving of dead hair, with a bleak blew Nose, over a chafeing-dish of starv'd Embers and Dining behind a Traverse Rag, in a shop no bigger than a Bird-cage,—go, go, starve again, do, do.

SIR SAMPSON, FROM CONGREVE'S *LOVE FOR LOVE*

You're an illiterate Fool, and I'm another, and the Stars are Lyars; and if I had Breath enough, I'd curse them and you, my self and every Body—Oons, Cully'd, bubbl'd, Jilted, woman-bobb'd at last—I have not Patience.

Cants

LADY PLYANT, FROM CONGREVE'S *DOUBLE DEALER*

You are so obliging, Sir ... So well bred ... So well drest, so boon mein, so eloquent, so unaffected, so easie, so free, so particular, so agreeable ... So gay, so graceful, so good teeth, so fine shape, so fine limbs, so fine linen, and I don't doubt but you have a very good skin, Sir.

CARELESS, FROM *THE DOUBLE DEALER*

Ah why are you so Fair, so bewitching Fair? O let me grow to the ground here, and feast upon that hand; O let me press it to my heart, my aking trembling heart, the nimble movement shall instruct your Pulse, and teach it to allarm Desire ... And must you leave me! Rather let me Languish out a Wretched Life, and breathe my Soul beneath your Feet ... O Heaven! I can't out-live this Night without your favor.

WAITWELL, FROM CONGREVE'S *WAY OF THE WORLD*

My Impatience Madam, is the effect of my transport;—and till I have the possession of your adoreable Person, I am tantaliz'd on a rack; And do but hang Madam, on the tenter of Expectation ... Dear Madam ... you are all Camphire and Frankincense, all Chastity and Odour.

SCENE ANALYSIS

Following is an analysis of the same scene from Congreve's *Way of the World* that received analysis at the end of Chapter 2. At this point, the scene will be analyzed with respect to the characters' use of wit and the devices of wit; the analysis will also function to demonstrate the differences between the wit of the true wits and that of the false wits.

Mirabell, Witwoud, Millamant, Mrs. Fainall, and Mincing, from Congreve's *Way of the World*

MIRABELL: You seem to be unattended, Madam—You us'd to have the Beau-mond Throng after you; and a Flock of gay fine Perrukes hovering round you.
[*As Mirabell walks in St. James Park with Mrs. Fainall, he greets his love, Millamant, whom he sees approaching. The greeting is devoid of any warm sentiment, Mirabell teasing Millamant as he refers to her custom of going abroad with an entire entourage composed mostly of fops.*]

WITWOUD: Like Moths about a Candle—I had like to have lost my Comparison for want of breath.
[*The fop Witwoud, who is walking with Millamant, does not allow her a retort, but rather responds to Mirabell immediately with a insipid similitude.*]

MILLAMANT: O I have deny'd my self Airs to Day. I have walk'd as fast through the Crowd—
[*Millamant, not to be denied a turn at a witty retort, immediately picks up on Witwoud's idea of being out of breath, and offers a play on the word "airs," suggesting being both out of breath and not putting on airs. The ball would be quickly returned to Mirabell, but Millamant is interrupted.*]

WITWOUD: As a Favourite in disgrace; and with as few Followers.
[*Although Millamant attempts to return the volley to Mirabell, Witwoud intercepts. Ignorant of or not heading the love battle that should be ensuing between Millamant and Mirabell, he completes the second half of a similitude that Millamant began.*]

MILLAMANT: Dear Mr. Witwoud, truce with your Similitudes; For I am as sick of 'em—
[*Millamant attempts to put an end to Witwoud's similitudes, of which she is growing tired, so that her encounter with Mirabell may continue. However, in attempting to quiet Witwoud, she begins yet another similitude.*]

WITWOUD: As a Phisician of a good Air—I cannot help it Madam, tho' 'tis against myself.
[*As Witwoud himself notes, he cannot control himself in completing another's similitudes. The ball is kept in play, but the true battle of wit is being thwarted*]

by a fool. However, his retort is quite witty, picking up on Millamant's use of "sick," and Witwoud is being facetious by implying that she is not at all sick of his similitudes since a physician would welcome "a good air."]

MILLAMANT: Yet again! Mincing, stand between me and his Wit.

[Millamant, seemingly at her wit's end, orders her woman to shield her from Witwoud's similitudes by personifying them and ordering Mincing to protect her from them.]

WITWOUD: Do Mrs. Mincing, like a Skreen before a great Fire. I confess I do blaze to Day, I am too bright.

[Witwoud, who is clearly out of control and lacking in true social grace, continues with yet another—this time insipid—similitude. Further, he clearly is not only reveling in his own wit but also flaunting it. He cleverly plays on the word "fire," suggesting that Millamant needs to be shielded from his cleverness, for it burns brightly this day.]

MRS. FAINALL: But dear Millamant, why were you so long?

[Mrs. Fainall abruptly puts an end to all witty volleys—insipid or otherwise— and cuts through with a direct question to Millamant.]

MILLAMANT: Long! Lord, have I not made violent haste? I have ask'd every living thing I met for you; I have enquir'd after you, as after a new Fashion.

[Millamant may be somewhat derailed by the question, retorting that she was in a "violent" hurry to meet Mrs. Fainall, referring back to Witwoud's earlier suggestion that he was out of breath following Millamant. However, being a true wit, she resorts to politeness, even gaiety, by creating a delightful similitude. She implies that she was as interested in Mrs. Fainall's whereabouts as she would be in a new fashion.]

WITWOUD: Madam, truce with your Similitudes—No, you met her Husband and did not ask him for her.

[Witwoud, again demonstrating his lack of true social grace, disagrees with Millamant and also uses her own words in stopping her use of similitudes.]

MILLAMANT: By your leave Witwoud, that were like enquiring after an old Fashion, to ask a Husband for his Wife.

[Millamant, an exemplar of social grace and true wit, is not in the least deterred and skillfully returns the volley with a brilliant similitude. Typical to sentiment of the time and to her own character, Millamant expresses how disdainful it is for a husband and wife to be so involved with each other's affairs that they would know of each other's whereabouts. It would be as uncouth as to pursue an out-of-date fashion. Further, she continues her own previous similitude by offering an antithesis to her previous use of "new Fashion."]

WITWOUD: Hum, a hit, a hit, a palpable hit, I confess it.

[Witwoud is so taken with her dexterity, he relinquishes the round, admitting defeat in the language of a fencer.]

MRS. FAINALL: You were dress'd before I came abroad.
[Mrs. Fainall is determined not to play the game and is trying to corner Millamant.]

MILLAMANT: Ay, that's true—O but then I had—Mincing what had I? Why was I so long?
[Millamant may be at a loss, Mrs. Fainall seeming to get the better of her. However, Millamant cleverly turns the problem over to Mincing, confident that she will rescue her. In doing so, she refuses to give in to the sincerity of Mrs. Fainall, refusing to indulge in any expression of true sentiment.]

MINCING: O Mem, your Laship staid to peruse a Pecquet of Letters.
[A true good servant, she has no trouble fabricating a cover for her mistress.]

MILLAMANT: O ay, Letters—I had Letters—I am persecuted with Letters—I hate Letters—No Body knows how to write Letters; and yet one has 'em, one does not know why—They serve one to pin up one's Hair.
[Clearly she is dissembling and being ever-so-delightful in doing so. Millamant has no intention of being put at a disadvantage. She seizes the opportunity to rail against letters, suggesting they are not good for anything except for rolling up and using to curl one's hair, as was the custom to do with paper.]

WITWOUD: Is that the way? Pray Madam, do you pin up your Hair with all your Letters? I find I must keep Copies.
[The fop Witwoud is also in love with Millamant and most likely writes volumes of tedious prose and poetry. He is chagrined to think his literary feats are being destroyed.]

MILLAMANT: Only with those in Verse, Mr. Witwoud. I never pin up my Hair with Prose. I fancy ones Hair wou'd not curl if it were pinn'd up with Prose. I think I try'd once Mincing.
[Again, never to be "one down," Millamant fashions a clever answer to Witwoud's inquiry, suggesting that only verse could "curl one's hair"—an ambiguous response.]

MINCING: O Mem, I shall never forget it.

MILLAMANT: Ay, poor Mincing tift and tift all morning.

MINCING: 'Till I had the Cremp in my Fingers I'll vow Mem. And all to no purpose. But When you Laship pins it up with Poetry, it sits so pleasant the next Day as any Thing, and is so pure and crips.
[Millamant is clearly enjoying the diversion with her maid, which not only diverts attention from Mrs. Fainall's probing but also demonstrates indifference to her lover, Mirabell.]

WITWOUD: Indeed, so crips?
[In true fopish style, Witwoud draws attention to Mincing's uneducated manner of speaking.]

MINCING: You're such a Critick, Mr. Witwoud.

MILLAMANT: Mirabell, Did not you take Exceptions last Night?—
O ay, and went away—Now I think on't I'm angry—No now I think
on't I'm pleased—For I believe I gave you some Pain.
[Being careful to maintain the upper hand by not allowing Mirabell to initiate an exchange, and growing tired of the diversion with Mincing, Millamant directs her attention, finally, to her lover. She refers to Mirabell's departure from her house the previous night, when he was clearly upset that she and her entourage of two fops and Millamant's aunt, old Lady Wishfort, at first ignored Mirabell and then railed against long visits. Further, she scores several points by putting Mirabell at the disadvantage, not allowing him to express his anger by catching him off guard—first by declaring she is angry with him and then by flaunting her pleasure in causing him pain.]

MIRABELL: Do's that please you?
[Not returning the ball through a clever retort, he resorts to a direct question, which usually puts the speaker at a disadvantage.]

MILLAMANT: Infinitely; I love to give Pain.
[She maintains the lead by dissembling.]

MIRABELL: You wou'd affect a Cruelty which is not in your Nature;
your true Vanity is in the power of pleasing.
[Mirabell seems to attempt to rely on expression of sincerity; however, he turns the tables on Millamant by declaring that Millamant's vanity lies in her power to please. This alludes to her vanity associated with her looks and bearing.]

MILLAMANT: O I ask your Pardon for that—One's Cruelty is one's
Power, and when one parts with one's Cruelty, one parts with one's
Power; and when one has parted with that, I fancy one's Old and Ugly.
[Millamant skillfully returns the volley, scoring several points with a brilliant, three-part, witty epigram. She contradicts Mirabell, asserting that her true power is her cruelty, which she possesses because of her youth and good looks.]

MIRABELL: Ay, ay, suffer your Cruelty to ruin the object of your Power,
to destroy your Lover—And then how vain, how lost a thing you'll
be! Nay, 'tis true: you are no longer handsome when you've lost your
Lover; your Beauty dies upon the Instant; For Beauty is the Lover's
Gift; 'tis he bestows your Charms—Your Glass is all a Cheat. The
Ugly and the Old, whom the Looking-glass mortifies, yet after Commendation can be flatter'd by it, and discover Beauties in it: For that
reflects Our Praises, rather than your Face.

[Mirabell, a keen player in the love battle of wit, immediately takes control of the game by fashioning a witty, complex epigrammatic retort. After Millamant asserts that a woman loses her power when she is old and ugly, Mirabell's retort is that women lose their power when they destroy their lover since their beauty is bestowed upon them by their lovers. Mirrors lie, and even when one is old and the mirror's reflection is mortifying, a lover can re-create one's beauty through flattery.]

MILLAMANT: O the Vanity of these Men! Fainall, dee hear him? If they did not commend us, we were not handsome! Now you must know they could not commend one, if one was not handsome. Beauty the Lover's Gift—Lord, what is a lover, that it can give? Why one makes Lovers as fast as one pleases, and they live as long as one pleases, and they die as soon as one pleases; And then if one pleases, one makes more.

[Millamant receives the ball and does not fumble. In fact, she laughs or makes fun of Mirabell's reasoning. She shoots down his assertion that a woman's lover could hold so much power. Epigrammatically, she undermines the importance of a lover by claiming that a woman creates lovers, and their tenures are as long as she allows. Further, when one love affair dies, she creates another at her whim.]

WITWOUD: Very pretty. Why you make no more of making of Lovers, Madam, than of making so many Card-matches.

[Witwoud acknowledges Millamant's victory of the volley and supports her contention that her "making of lovers" is of little significance to her by aptly comparing it with a game of cards. Witwoud is a fan in the grandstands, so to speak, urging on his favorite player. Note that both characters support the need for the lady to feign indifference to love.]

MILLAMANT: One no more owes one's Beauty to a Lover, than one's Wit to an Eccho: They can but reflect what we look and say; vain empty things if we are silent or unseen, And want a being.

[Millamant does not acknowledge Witwoud and quickly goes for more points by continuing her contention through the creation of a witty epigram. Lovers, like echoes, can only reflect what is already there. Further, lovers and echoes are merely empty or vain if the lady does not speak well nor show herself; further, she suggests that if it weren't for the lady, they would lack existence. She turns Mirabell's original contention around on him.]

MIRABELL: Yet to those two vain empty things, you owe two of the greatest Pleasures of Your Life.

[Mirabell serves the ball, setting himself up for the upper hand, knowing that Millamant must question him.]

MILLAMANT: How so?
[Millamant falls into his trap by asking the necessary question, clearly allowing him to score a point.]

MIRABELL: To your Lover you owe the pleasure of hearing your selves prais'd; and to an Eccho the pleasures of hearing your selves talk.
[Having been asked the question he anticipated, Mirabell scores several points by asserting that two of women's greatest pleasures are hearing themselves praised by their lovers and hearing themselves talk.]

WITWOUD: But I know a Lady that loves talking so incessantly, she won't give an Eccho fair play; she has that everlasting Rotation of Tongue, that an Eccho must wait till she dies, before it can catch her last Words.
[Witwoud interrupts, attempting to take the battle into his own court by challenging Mirabell's contention.]

MILLAMANT: O Fiction; Fainall, let us leave these Men.
[Millamant tires of the game and feigns indifference to it, perhaps because of Mirabell's previous points. However, she takes control by overturning the checkerboard and thereby ends the game.]

NOTES

1. Joan Wildeblood, *The Polite World: A Guide to English Manners and Deportment* (London: Davis-Poynter, 1973), p. 92.
2. Quoted in Bonamy Dobree, *Restoration Comedy 1660–1720* (London: Oxford University Press, 1924), p. 37.
3. *Marriage a la Mode* (Works, IV), Dedication, pp. 253–54. Quoted in Kathleen M. Lynch, *The Social Mode of Restoration Comedy* (New York: Octagon, 1965), p. 139.
4. John Dryden, the Author's Apology Prefixed to *The State of Innocence and Fall of Man* (1677), Ker, I, p. 190. Quoted in R. C. Sharma, *Themes and Conventions in the Comedy of Manners* (New York: Asia, 1965), p. 263.

4

USING THE VOICE

INTRODUCTION

It was noted in the previous chapter that the rules associated with social manners and etiquette in the upper echelon of seventeenth-century
British society "attained a zenith of artificial complexity."[1] A hallmark
of this complexity was keen verbal dexterity, which was flaunted by the
fashionable world of the time. As we have seen in a study of the language
and literary devices, the plays are a celebration of this complexity and
dexterity. Thus, it follows that in performance, the vocal expression of
such artificial complexity must be a major consideration. It is difficult
to imagine, for instance, that such extravagant use of artificial devices
of speech, replete with witty epigrams, similitudes, verbal warfare, rant,
and cant, can be delivered in the style of contemporary film acting. The
shooting down of another's similitude with one's own or the topping or
undercutting of another character's lines require at least a basic understanding of the use and power of pitch or melodic changes, for example.
The narrow pitch range that characterizes most camera acting, as well as
much theatrical realism, is not sufficient for playing the highly adorned
language in the comedies of manners. Further, the less precise nature
of diction and articulation associated with much contemporary realism
will also not serve the performance of such sparkling dialogue. Additionally, imagery, similitudes, epigrams, and all devices must be colored with
the voice and created in such a way that their syntax is readily under-
standable. The actor must have a good basic sense—or develop one—of

creating verbal syntax, or at least be capable of deciphering the *operative words* in this artifice-laden dialogue.

This chapter, then, supplies a variety of tools toward approaching the vocal delivery of the texts (particularly the language of the true wits and the false wits), so that the language may sparkle at the center of the performance of these plays. It should be noted that the topic of dialects will not be covered in this book. Today, more and more American companies are producing these British comedies utilizing standard American speech, as the British dialects are often deemed unnecessary in this country. Further, to thoroughly delineate and teach a dialect requires quite a commitment in print. If a dialect is desired, there are many valuable instructional texts and tapes available.

The chapter will approach the use of the voice in performance of these comedies by focusing on the following components: (1) operative words; (2) imagistic techniques; (3) the vocal variables of pitch, rhythm, and tempo; and (4) playing the sounds. The chapter concludes with an analysis of the passage analyzed at the end of Chapters 2 and 3. In this case, the scene will be analyzed with respect to potential vocal and speech choices for playing the text.

UNDERSTANDING OPERATIVE WORDS

Operative words is a term that many a director readily throws around at rehearsal, often dumbfounding many a young or inexperienced actor. With contemporary American society's penchant for emphasizing nonoperative words in conversation, it is no wonder that most young actors fail at the task when instructed to "play the operative words." Quite simply, playing the operative words entails delivering text in such a manner that the words instrumental to creating understanding or meaning are emphasized in some way through the use of the components of vocal delivery: pitch or melody, tempo, rhythm, dynamics, and, of course, diction and articulation. Further, the words that are not instrumental in creating understanding or meaning are de-emphasized. Emphasis can be achieved through any of the vocal components, such as pitch changes, rhythmic elongation, and dynamic changes (getting louder or becoming softer), or by using more than one component at the same time. That is, a speaker may emphasize a word through both pitch and volume. The specifics of employing the various components or *variables of speech* will be treated separately under the subsequent headings in this chapter.

A good starting point, however, is to gain an overall understanding of operative words. It is not a difficult task to decipher the operatives in any phrase. Usually, it takes no more than developing sensitivity toward identifying which words in any sentence or phrase are integral to revealing meaning and which are not. For example, when someone instructs another, "Hurry to the store for milk! The guests will arrive in five minutes," it is quite clear that prepositions and articles are of little importance to the listener. Nouns and verbs are usually of key significance, such as "hurry," "store," "milk," "guests," "arrive," and "five minutes" (considering this unit of time as one noun). Further, within this list, there is also a hierarchy. The listener is clear that he must go to a "store," and he is most likely aware of the fact that "guests" will "arrive," making these operative words less important than others within the phrase. Therefore, the key operative words are "hurry," "milk," and "five minutes," the listener capable of gleaning meaning from these alone. These words must be emphasized by using one or more of the components of vocal delivery. Accordingly, the other words of less importance must be downplayed.

To the beginner, it may seem quite a leap from deciphering operative words in such a simple contemporary phrase as "Hurry to the store," to doing so in "the World is but a constant Keeping Gallant, whom we fail not to quarrel with, when any thing crosses us, yet cannot part with't for our hearts" (Eliza, in *The Plain Dealer*). However, as previously implied, a sensitivity to operative words can be readily developed in a surprisingly short time when dealing with the texts of the comedies. The texts are not written in, or replete with allusions to, archaic English. Rather, even though highly adorned, they are written in modern English and are typically quite logical in construction. However, the syntactical structure of the thoughts tends to be more complex than in contemporary conversation. By achieving simple familiarity with the texts, one may become more sensitive to the syntactical structures and to the identification of operative words.

Before delving into some analysis of excerpts from the texts of the plays, it is also important to understand that any consideration of operative words within such ornamented language must take into account the artifice itself. That is, much like in poetry, many of the words and phrases exist to expand an image or thought, or quite simply for the purpose of adornment itself. Therefore, in choosing words or phrases to emphasize in performance, we cannot consider only words that convey meaning. Since the art of conversation, with its sparkling, witty dialogue, was highly prized within seventeenth-century upper-class society, a contemporary performer of the comedies cannot downplay all words and phrases that seem to exist solely for the purpose of adornment rather than for the conveyance of meaning. To better understand this concept, it will prove helpful at this point to analyze a few passages from the previous chapter, which reveal some of the devices and practices utilized in the language of the texts. This simple analysis will demonstrate which words should be emphasized or "played up" to convey meaning and which should be emphasized to display facility with language or to flaunt a keen wit.

An excellent way in which to commence an analysis of operative words is to consider similitudes, as their comparative structure and their conciseness provide a simple format for identifying the important words or phrases within a thought. As the audience becomes accustomed to the language and thought structures in the comedies, it becomes quite attuned to the similitudes, eventually realizing that someone or something is going to be compared to someone or something else. Thus, the audience listens for the main information in these comparisons: that is, *what* or *whom* is being compared to *what* or *whom*, and in *what* manner. The brief, previously cited exchange from *Love in a Wood* serves well to demonstrate this.

RANGER: Incredulous envy; thou art as envious, as an impotent Letcher at a Wedding.

VINCENT: Thou are either mad, or as vain as a French-man, newly return'd home from a Campaign, or obliging England.

RANGER: Thou art as envious as a Rival.

Ranger, intent on proving that Vincent is envious of his previous night's engagement with a woman, is not content with merely calling Vincent "envious." His point is driven home with similitudes, thereby proving himself a keen player in the game of bantering. He commences with an explication, setting up the topic of discussion to be bantered. Since his opener is an explication, both words must be emphasized ("Incredulous" and "envy"), but the subject is more important than its descriptive adjective. Therefore, "envy" must be primarily played. It is quite clear that Ranger is calling Vincent envious, so the second-person pronoun "thou," as well as "art" and "as" that follow, may be downplayed. As mentioned, the audience has already attuned its ears to these comparisons. "Envious" is pointed, though not as much as the first derivation of the word "envy," since it is a repetition. The next important or operative phrase is the colorful image Ranger provides to complete his similitude. ("As" and "an" may be downplayed since the listener is quite aware that this is a comparison and that a similitude is on the way.) "Impotent," "Letcher," and "Wedding" must all be played up in order to convey the keen humor of this image, for one is indeed hard-pressed to find a man so envious as an "impotent Letcher at a Wedding." (Obviously, "at" and "a" need to be downplayed.) There can be, however, three different degrees of emphasis within the three words responsible for creating the image. The noun "Letcher" is the anchor in this thought, with the adjective "impotent" strengthening the image in this similitude. The colorful image is then further fortified with the noun "Wedding." Thus, one could feasibly play up "Letcher" the most, followed in importance by "impotent," and finally, "Wedding."

Vincent responds, first seemingly not willing to commit to the game of similitude making, but then by creating a similitude denigrating the French. (Feasibly, nothing is so vain as a Frenchman who has just returned from a foreign war or from some affair in which he "obliged" or accommodated England with his presence, with a strong sexual suggestion in this word choice.) Aware that he is referring to Ranger, the first operative word is "either," which suggests there will be more to follow, and the second—and more important—one is "mad." One then gets hit with the similitude, which emphasizes "vain French-man," "newly return'd," "Campaign," and "obliging England." Through these words, the image is solidified. Ranger then neatly sums up the exchange and wins the point by cleverly noting his friend is as "envious as a Rival." After all, he just competed with Ranger in his battle of similitudes. In this final line, "Rival" is obviously key, with the repeated "envious" of secondary importance.

The epigrams, or concise pithy sayings, are also clearly demonstrative of how meaning is conveyed through the emphasis of operative words. In merely listing the operative words from a previously cited epigram, it is surprising how readily the overall meaning can be gleaned:

> Woman . . . marries . . . love better
> . . . much mistaken
> Wencher . . . marries . . . live better.
> . . . marrying . . . encrease love
> . . . gaming . . . become rich
> . . . loose . . . little stock . . . had

If an actor truly emphasizes these words through one or more of the vocal variables, the meaning of the epigram from *The Country Wife* is made clear to such an extent that even if one or more of the nonoperatives is dropped or inaudible, the audience will receive Lucy's meaning:

> The Woman that marries to love better, will be as much mistaken, as the Wencher that marries to live better. No, Madam, marrying to encrease love, is like gaming to become rich; alas you only loose what little stock you had before.

As with the similitude, an audience will become accustomed to these little bits of moralizing and the related syntactical construction. Most epigrams rely on some sort of comparison (many, in fact, contain similitudes), but their cumulative effect is the conveyance of an aphorism or pithy saying. Therefore, the audience will progressively listen for the comparisons being made and retain that information in order to hear the lesson. Thus, when Eliza admonishes Olivia, who says that she is weary of the world, through the actor's playing of the operative words, the audience can readily take in the comparison and wait for the lesson. That is, when the actor emphasizes the correct words and downplays the articles, prepositions, readily apparent pronouns, and any other repeated or unimportant words, and when the actor is cognizant of and plays the structure of the comparison followed by some sort of little lesson, meaning is conveyed. By playing the following operative words, Eliza's meaning becomes quite clear:

> ...World...constant Keeping Gallant,
> ...fail not...quarrel with
> ...any thing crosses
> ...cannot part...hearts.

("The World is but a constant Keeping Gallant, whom we fail not to quarrel with, when any thing crosses us, yet cannot part with't for our hearts.")

In this passage, "World" is important, but not as important as that which it is being compared to, particularly since it is a repeated word. (Olivia has just stated that she is weary of the "world.") The image created through alliteration, "constant Keeping Gallant," is very important—so powerful in what it evokes, it is difficult to downplay the adjectives and still create the image. This entire image should be played up as a little jewel of speech. In the next line, the first-person plural is implied, since Eliza is admonishing Olivia, but it is important that (we) women "fail not" (to) "quarrel with" this "constant Keeping Gallant," "quarrel" being the most important word in this phrase. Next, although "any thing" is the subject of the next phrase, it is not as important as "crosses," and "us" is even less important since it refers back to the first-person plural pronoun. The last phrase of the epigram is what solidifies the meaning and Eliza's lesson to Olivia. The transitional word "Yet" is not of much importance, but the verb phrase "cannot part" is of major significance, followed by the word "heart" as secondary in the hierarchy.

If the actor plays these operative words and plays the overall structure of the thought as well, meaning will be conveyed. This epigram is quite typical in structure to many in the texts of the comedies. First, there is the overall comparison; next follows some sort of qualifying information, usually some sort of parenthetical phrase or clause, which contains the important lesson, however. Thus, the actor must first vocally play the sound of "this equals that." If the subject, as in our example, is a repeated word, the sound of the phrase may be unbalanced, with the subject being less emphasized than that to which it is being compared. Otherwise, both may be of equal vocal intensity or color. The next section, in this case a parenthetical phrase, is the section of *additional information*, or that section which actually introduces the lesson or moral. Parenthetical phrases are usually downplayed vocally, and one may play an overall sense of undercutting the first part of the epigram while still playing the operative words, at least in all but the final portion of the epigram. The last short phrase, which delivers the punch line, must be played up at least to the degree of the initial statement.

Not all epigrams are structured with the lesson-containing portion as a parenthetical phrase or clause. Often, the comparison is followed immediately by the overall moral, such as in "marrying to encrease love, is like gaming to become rich; alas you only loose what little stock you had before." The lesson is written or structured as its own thought, not as additional information connected by *that, which*, or *whom*. Thus, there need not be any consideration of downplaying the parenthetical phrase; the actor need only to make sure that after the comparison is created, the lesson is solidified.

WORKING IMAGISTICALLY: UTILIZING LABAN'S COMPONENTS OF MOVEMENT FOR THE VOICE

It should be noted that any of the ensuing vocal work in this chapter should be preceded by a thorough vocal warm-up, which includes breath work, exercises in phonation or producing tone, and diction work, all incorporating the use of good posture. See Appendix A for suggested exercises for warming up the voice.

This section serves to provide an approach by which the student may be introduced and become sensitized to, as well as experiment with, the overall nature and sound of the language in Restoration comedies of manners in an *imagistic* way. The techniques will also be used in specific ways so that the student may attain an initial approach toward playing operative words and the overall structure of the thoughts.

At first, it might seem rather strange to utilize Rudolf Laban's theories of movement for any sort of vocal work. However, over the years, voice and movement teachers have recognized the many benefits of teaching either discipline from a more holistic approach that incorporates both voice and movement. Indeed, many colleges, universities, and other acting training programs have gone to this integrated approach. Beyond this, the eight *effort actions*, by which Laban defines or describes movement, provide an excellent basis for actors to think imagistically about their voices. This can be a wonderful adjunct to the more technical training required for the voice. Exploring the vocal sounds related to Laban's effort actions can serve as an exploration into timbral (tone color) capabilities of the voice. Further, the effort actions provide very tangible descriptions by which actors may describe or characterize the vocal qualities utilized in the various performance styles associated with the period styles and genre of theatrical literature.

In her book *Laban for Actors and Dancers*,[2] Jean Newlove provides a clear and concise description of Laban's movement theories and principles. This writer is greatly indebted to Newlove's thorough study and succinct, intelligent explanations. For those not familiar with Laban's work, before moving to the actual exercises, it is necessary to attain a basic understanding of a few of Laban's principles. What follows is only a brief description of what Laban saw to be the four major *motion factors* of all movement, as well as a breakdown of what he calls the eight effort actions.

Laban felt that four motion factors or *continuums* characterized or influenced all movement: *flow, space, time,* and *weight.* Flow suggests that movement can be *free* if it is uninterrupted; there are no stops. It is considered *bound* if the motion can be paused or stopped at any time before it continues. When considering space, the concept of whether or not movement is made directly toward a target is of concern. Does the body move in a *direct* or *indirect* manner toward a target? Laban viewed time in movement with respect to duration. That is, is a certain movement *sustained* over a period of time or is it *sudden?* With respect to weight, Laban noted that all movement occurs with either a *strong* or *light* force.

Based on these characterizations of movement, Laban devised eight effort actions, or eight different combinations of weight, time, and space. He labeled these as *Press, Glide, Punch, Dab, Slash, Flick, Wring,* and *Float.* The following is a description of each effort action, based on three of Laban's motion factors of space, time, and weight.

Press: Direct, Sustained, Strong
Glide: Direct, Sustained, Light
Punch: Direct, Sudden, Strong
Dab: Direct, Sudden, Light
Slash: Indirect, Sudden, Strong
Flick: Indirect, Sudden, Light
Wring: Indirect, Sustained, Strong
Float: Indirect, Sustained, Light

Exercises

Experimenting with Laban

LEARNING THE EIGHT EFFORT ACTIONS

The first exercise is a basic one in which the student may experiment with the eight effort actions through movement and voice. If students are not familiar with the Laban technique, it is suggested that each effort action be introduced and worked through in the sequential manner suggested here. If there is familiarity with the technique, then the student or the group may simply start improvising movement associated with any specific effort action and then layer in improvisation with the voice. If this is done, pay particular attention to the light effort actions. It should be noted that this basic Laban exercise will also function as the introductory exercise in the unit on movement. The four light actions will be the ones predominantly utilized in both the movement and vocal work for this period and genre. A step that utilizes recorded music has been incorporated into this overall exercise, as music provides a wonderful impulse for students to improvise with their bodies. It is strongly suggested that for the four effort actions that require a light force or weight, selections should be made from music of the period. The music of the following composers is suggested: Henry Purcell, Jean Baptiste Lully, Girolamo Frescobaldi, Claudio Monteverdi, Heinrich Shutz, Jan Pieters Sweelinck, and John Blow.

The process for the first effort action will be thoroughly delineated. After this, only the introduction to each action will be explained; the subsequent steps delineated under the first one should then be followed for each. While delineating the process for each effort action, suggested questions will be supplied for the actor to ask herself or for the group leader to provide during the process of exploration. These questions can be applied while experimenting with any of the actions.

Press

1. Imagine that there is a very large object that you are trying to push away from you, first, with your hands. You find the object is too heavy, so you start incorporating the entire arm, the shoulders, your entire side while engaging the abdominal muscles, your upper legs, lower legs, and feet, until your entire body is engaged in this action of pressing this heavy body or object away from you. Gradually, the object starts to move very slowly across the room. Make this your task: Move the imaginary object from one side of the room to the other. You may need to shift your weight; feature one part of the body then another; and take very short breaks to

restabilize yourself and start again. The important aspect is that you attempt to press this large object by utilizing as much of your body as possible. Remember, this movement is strong, sustained, and direct.

2. To any music that suggests the action of pressing, freely improvise movement around the room based on pressing. Be sure to experiment with all different parts of the body, at times utilizing perhaps only the feet, and at other times utilizing two or more parts at once.

3. While you're still moving, the music should fade out. While still exploring the Press with various parts of the body, start experimenting with vocal sound. Ask yourself the following questions: "What is the sound of my arms pressing?" "What is the sound of my torso pressing?" "What are the sounds of my hands and head pressing?" "What is a strong, sustained, direct sound?" Try adding sound to as many different ways of pressing as possible.

4. After this experiment, you may wish to add the following: Improvise until you find a movement phrase based on pressing. Then add on a sound or series of sounds that correspond to this movement. Next, let the sound evolve into a short verbal phrase, one that is meaningful or one that is purely nonsensical. Continue with this movement and phrase, and try several others.

Glide

1. The overall sensation of the Glide can be imagined readily through recalling or imagining the sensation of roller- or ice-skating, or of in-line skating. You may wish to first simply glide around the room as if skating. Then, adding music, start experimenting with gliding the hands and arms, the upper body, the legs and feet, whole lower body, and so on. Experience moving and making sound that is sustained, light, and direct. Be sure to ask yourself what this light, sustained movement does to the pitch and duration of your vocal work. Continue with the other aspects of the exercise delineated in steps 2 through 4 of the previous exercise.

Punch

1. The Punch is readily kinesthetically recognized through the action of throwing a punch into the air. Experiment with all parts of the body, singularly and in unison. For example, punch with the head, punch with the feet, punch with the torso, or punch with a foot and the head. Move and make a sound that is strong, sudden, and direct. Be sure to focus on the force and the suddenness of the sound. Continue with the other aspects of the exercise.

Dab

1. The Dab can be recognized by performing the action of dabbing at a spot on your face. Imagine that you are dabbing on ointment or lip balm, or gently dabbing tears off your face. Experiment with all parts of the body and move and make a sound that is light, sudden, and direct. With respect to sound, where in your body does this light, sudden sound seem to originate? Where does it sit pitch-wise? What happens to your breathing when you emit such short, light sounds? Continue with the other aspects of the exercise.

Slash

1. An indirect, sudden and strong movement, the Slash can be recognized by imagining and miming that you are holding a machete and are slashing your way through a heavy growth of vegetation by which you are surrounded. Again, be sure to go beyond this obvious one and experiment with all parts of the body. Be careful to note that the Slash is strong but does not have a definite target. It is, therefore, a somewhat wild, uncontrolled gesture, and an interesting one with which to experiment vocally. Where, for instance, does the Slash "live" in the voice? How much breath power does it require? Perform the other aspects of the exercise.

Flick

1. The Flick is also sudden and indirect, but it is light in weight. Imagine and mime that you have an insect on you that will certainly bite or sting you if it is left there. Squashing it would not be a good choice; flick it off your body. Continue the exercise, asking yourself (or with the instructor asking) a variety of questions referring to the lightness, suddenness, and indirect quality of this motion. How do the feet, the torso, the head, the shoulders, the pelvis, and so on respond to the Flick? What kind of sound is inspired by the Flick? Where does it seem to resonate in the internal resonators? How many different vowel sounds seem to work for the Flick, and which ones do not? Complete the other aspects of the exercise.

Wring

1. Imagine that you are at the beach and that a child in your care has dragged his towel into the surf. It is now time to depart. Bend over and pick up the sodden, very large towel, and with all your upper-body strength while firmly grounding yourself with your lower body, commence wringing it out. Feel the weight of the towel and experience the intense muscular effort required to perform this task. While experimenting with other parts of the body, the

experience may not be very similar to the motion of wringing out a towel. Focus on the constriction or engagement of the muscles involved in the wringing of various parts of the body. Vocally, what are the strange, even ugly, sounds that are inspired by this strong, indirect, sustained movement? Where do they seem to "live" in the body? Can you produce these ugly, tense sounds with consonants? Continue with the other components of the exercise.

Float

1. Bend over from the waist, letting your fingers dust the floor, and imagine that you are slowly filling with helium from your toes up. You are a giant balloon to be used in a parade. Let your body slowly fill with helium, allowing yourself to become extremely light and buoyant during the process. Keep filling until your arms and hands rise up over your head and your entire body drifts aimlessly about the room. Imagine that you suddenly catch gentle breezes or gusts of wind that carry you very lightly one way or another. Maintain a feeling of weightlessness that keeps you up on your toes and moving in a very sustained manner without direction. Continue with all aspects of the exercise, allowing different parts of the body to lead at different times. Experience the lightness of sound that drifts from your body and observe how this sound "lives" somewhere altogether different from the Wring. How much air is required to emit these sounds? Are the sounds loud or soft?

COMBINING THE EFFORT ACTIONS

After working through all eight actions individually, it is a valuable exercise to combine two or three actions, working various parts of the body with the voice.

1. Choose any of the eight effort actions and start moving freely about the room, inspired by this action. Start finding a sound to accompany this movement, still moving freely about the space. Now choose a secondary action, which will enter into your movement at any time. It is best not to predict when this will happen. Devise a sound for this action too. If possible, while still moving and phonating, inspired by your primary action, and layering in a secondary, attempt to layer in a tertiary. Try to maintain a hierarchy.

2. Choose any one of the eight actions and let it inspire movement for one specific part of your body. Identify a sound to accompany this movement. Discover movement and sound as you move about the space. Next, choose another action that will inspire a different

part of the body, all the while maintaining the first. Be sure to discover a different sound for this action. Keep building on as much as you can, maintaining each movement and sound associated with each specific body part you choose. For example, the legs (with the voice) press, the arms and the hands (with the voice) float, and the head (with the voice) dabs.

Using Laban for Working Voice and Text

Considering what we know about the language of the texts of the comedies, particularly that of the true wits and false wits, and holding up Laban's template, so to speak, it seems readily apparent that there are four actions on which the student will want to focus: the Glide, the Dab, the Flick, and the Float. These actions, all on the light side of the weight spectrum, are most suitable for this highly adorned language of the true wits and the false wits. When characters speak in similitudes, create colorful imagery and metaphors, or engage in epigrammatic speech, the voice must move quickly and lightly through these devices of wit. Further, when engaging in the volleys of repartee and sparkling love battles, speakers must be "light on their feet" to keep the ball in play. Generally speaking, the strong actions would impede the forward motion of the game. It is easy to imagine a character flicking off one similitude after another, or elegantly dabbing a witty retort back to her challenger. A character may glide through a complexly constructed passage or may float a cant while feigning love to a gullible fop. This is not to say that the strong actions should be avoided altogether and are useless in these texts. Although the lighter actions suit the refined and ornamented conversation, the strong actions will supply necessary contrast. For instance, a character might slip into the Press when delivering a bit of bawdy conversation. A fop's rant might be based predominantly on the Slash or the Punch; and perhaps the Wring might be the basis for a bit of stinging raillery. Further, a character may generally rely on one light action for the majority of a sentence but slip in a strong one now and then to stress an operative word. Finally, the language of the witless may be executed utilizing predominantly the heavy effort actions.

LABAN AND TEXT 1

A good opener for using the effort actions on text is to choose any passage from the comedies and start moving and speaking with one effort action of light weight. Any of the text found in step 3 in the exercise "Relishing the Words" in Chapter 3 will suffice. It is best to be memorize these passages for this exercise. Then start layering in a secondary action, and then a tertiary, one or both of which may be from the strong list. At this point, try not to predict on which word or words you will change to a different action. For example, when improvising on Lady Wishfort's brief monologue, one may rely on the Float, with a secondary emphasis on the Glide. Perhaps the Press might sneak in now and then. Improvise on these passages several times, trying different combinations of the actions, keeping a light action primary.

As an alternative, to experiment with the text of the witless, use any of the same text, but choose one of the strong effort actions to be primary. Then layer in secondary and tertiary actions, both from the list of light actions.

LABAN AND TEXT 2—OPERATIVE WORDS

Now, using these same passages, take some time to mark or highlight what you feel to be the operative words in the text you have chosen. Be careful to highlight or underline only those that are absolutely integral to creating meaning and those that are decorative in nature. Remember to avoid repetitions or anything that is understood. Again, choose your primary light action, as well as secondary and tertiary ones from either the light or strong list. Practice the passage, and each time you come to a highlighted word, rely on your secondary or tertiary action. It is beneficial to practice speaking the text while both moving about the room and also using very little movement.

Again, experimenting with using the voice for the witless can be achieved by selecting a strong effort action as primary and emphasizing the operative words with the secondary and tertiary choices of at least one from the light side of the list.

LABAN AND TEXT 3—SIMILITUDES AND EPIGRAMS

This exercise is similar to the previous one. After all, speaking similitudes or epigrams effectively requires a sensitivity to playing the operative words. Experiment with the various similitudes and epigrams created by the several characters from the comedies that are found in Chapter 3 in the second and third sets of exercises. It may suffice merely to improvise directly with these passages, trying different combinations of the actions. Through merely experimenting with several passages, the student will become more and more confident with identifying and highlighting the operative words. Or, you may choose to first highlight the words or phrases you wish to set off with secondary or tertiary actions and then practice these passages as you have marked them.

It is also important to aurally create the structure or syntax of the similitudes. For example, attempt to find the balance in your voice to balance the construction of the thought. That is, repetition of a sound inspired by a certain effort action may create this sense of aural balance. Further, if there is a sense of verbal surprise in the passage, set this off with your secondary or tertiary choice. Consider the following similitude spoken by Witwoud in *The Way of the World*:

> Friendship without Freedom is as dull as Love without enjoyment, or wine without toasting.

In construction, this similitude could be described as an "A equals B and also C" construction. That is, "Friendship without Freedom" equals "Love without enjoyment," and it also equals "wine without toasting." This needs to be heard in how the actor plays the structure with his voice. Perhaps "Friendship without," "Love without" and "wine without" are all inspired by the same action, and the indirect objects ("Freedom," "enjoyment," and "toasting") are all spoken with a secondary action in mind. Because the phrase is a short list and the speaker may want to drive his point home with the second comparison, the final indirect object ("toasting") could be spoken based on the third action.

Similarly, find the vocal balance, and then the oppositions, when speaking epigrams. Consider one spoken by Horner in *The Country Wife*:

> Mistresses are like books; if you pore upon them too much, they doze you, and Make you unfit for company; but if us'd discreetly, you are the fitter for Conversation for them.

Find the balance in sound, perhaps by aligning the similitude with the conditional phrase and the result. That is, the subject "Mistresses" may be initiated by the same effort action as the first conditional phrase, and the comparison to books may be the same as "they doze you" and "Make you unfit for company." The second conditional phrase may also sound like the subject, and the final result may rely on the tertiary action. For example, one solution may look like this:

Mistresses are like	=	Glide
books	=	Dab
if you pore upon them too much	=	Glide
they doze you, and Make you unfit for company	=	Dab
but if us'd discreetly	=	Glide
you are the fitter for Conversation for them	=	Slash

LABAN AND TEXT 4—VERBAL BATTLES AND BANTERING

As mentioned, in order to keep the energy moving forward in the keen verbal battles between the true wits, the light actions are generally most suitable. Before moving into the text, you might wish to practice the first exercise under "Verbal Battles and Bantering" from Chapter 3, in which partners engage in a verbal battle using limited vocabularies and alliteration. Play either a primary action only, or both a primary and a secondary. For example, try using only a light action, two light ones, or one light and one strong. At all costs, use the Glide, the Dab, the Flick, and the Float to keep the game moving forward.

Now, with a partner, practice this dexterity on a bit of text, using any of the short scenes from the previous chapter that demonstrate wit, raillery, love battles, or dissembling. First, choose an overall action and practice the volley with your partner. Next, layer in one or two more effort actions and vocally highlight operative words with these. You may wish to start by just standing or sitting, letting the action influence the voice only. Or, you may start moving about the space, letting the primary action work on your body. You may wish to ease into the text by first phonating sound without words, eventually starting the dialogue when you are in *communion* with your partner. Continue to move about the space, letting the effort actions influence both your body and your voice.

Here, too, the voice and language of the witless may be explored by reversing the hierarchy of the effort actions, making the heavy ones primary and the lighter actions secondary or tertiary, or both.

THE VOCAL VARIABLES OF PITCH, RHYTHM, AND TEMPO

What are being referred to as the *vocal variables of speech* are actually no more than the components of all music: pitch, rhythm, tempo, dynamics, and timbre or tone color. Like the sound of music performed by any melodic instrument, the human speaking voice cannot be void of any of these. A voice may have a limited pitch range but cannot be without pitch. The same holds true for rhythm, tempo, and dynamics. The voice may not demonstrate much diversity in these, but it cannot be completely devoid of these variables. Rather, every human voice has its own tone color, or timbre, as do instruments. Beyond this, it can be said that each consonant and vowel has its own inherent timbre. Thus, the human voice can never be lacking timbre. However, an accomplished speaking voice must exceed the natural occurrence of the variables and demonstrate facility in them.

This section will focus on pitch, rhythm, and tempo for the purposes of playing the language of the comedies. Dynamics (or the varying degree of loud and soft) is probably the most readily understood variable and that which is most utilized by beginning actors; therefore, it will not be considered a primary tool toward vocal expressiveness in this section. Further, timbre, or tone color, is best addressed through the previously explained Laban-inspired exercises, as each effort action typically inspires the actor to make different timbral choices. It too will not be considered a primary tool in this section. Therefore, the focus will be on manipulating the variables of pitch, tempo, and rhythm as necessary skills and valuable tools for playing the sparkling language in the comedies of manners.

Pitch and Melody

The New Harvard Dictionary of Music initially defines pitch as

> the perceived quality of a sound that is chiefly a function of its fundamental frequency—the number of oscillations per second of the sounding object or of the particles of air excited by it . . . pitch is regarded as becoming higher with increasing frequency and lower with decreasing frequency.[3]

For the purposes of the actor, pitch can be understood simply as the varying degrees of *highs* and *lows* in the voice, or in other words, the varying frequencies. When the various pitches work together, or somehow sound as if they belong together, *melody* results. It is often pitch changes, or the melodic quality of one's voice, that account for the communication of much textual or subtextual meaning. For example, a person who is hysterical will most likely speak in a very high pitch range. Even if the listener cannot understand the words, the subtext is very clear. Beyond creating overall or generalized subtext, pitch changes are naturally used to highlight the operative words in our day-to-day interactions, providing the voice with melody. A parent commanding a recalcitrant child might emphasize the last word of this sentence through pitch inflection: "Go to the store—now!" Logically, the child might emphasize the second word of the following sentence through the same technique: "I won't go!" Additionally, often in polysyllabic words, the entire word will not be emphasized through inflection, but only the stressed syllable. For example, only the first syllable of "beautiful" might be inflected in the following sentence: "She wore a beautiful dress!" It must be noted, however, that a melodic voice is not one that indiscriminately changes pitch, for melody is defined by a sense of order, or of individual pitches working together. In the speaking voice, melody may be viewed as the frequent, but skillful, use of pitch change to create meaning and emphasis. Thus, for the purposes of acting the comedies, we will explore not only how pitch variation can be utilized to create meaning but also how it may bring the sparkling language to life.

Before the following exercises are performed, it is recommended that the student warm up with pitch exercises. The most thorough pitch warm-up can be achieved through the use of a piano or keyboard, if either is available. Humming or singing five-note scales on the various vowels, ascending a half-step for each new scale, is a wonderful traditional singing warm-up. If a keyboard or pianist is not available, again, refer to Appendix A for other exercises. Another excellent warm-up for pitch work is Kristen Linklater's exercise in working through the *resonators*.[4]

Exercises for Pitch

RECITATIVE EXERCISE—PART I

In operas or oratorios, the sections of vocal music that are more speech-like are referred to as *recitatives*. They are unlike *arias* in that they do not encompass a wide pitch range. They are not the songs within a work, so to speak. *The New Harvard Dictionary of Music* defines a recitative as

> a style of text setting that imitates and emphasizes the natural inflections, rhythms, and syntax of speech. Such a setting avoids extremes of pitch and intensity and repetition of words, allowing the music to be primarily a vehicle for the words.[5]

What is of significance here is that the music emphasizes the natural inflections and syntax of the speaking voice, which it does through rhythm, tempo, or pitch. Pitch-wise, since recitative operates in a very narrow range, the important words will be emphasized through wider pitch changes. Imagine that the phrase "She wore a beautiful dress" is to be sung as a recitative. Very simply, all syllables could be on the same note, with the first syllable of "beautiful" emphasized by singing any pitch quite a bit higher or lower than the rest of the sentence. Or, since this exercise is a singing improvisation, the entire word "beautiful" could be sung at the higher or lower pitch.

As a warm-up to singing excerpts from the texts, you may wish to choose sentences or phrases of contemporary English with which to experiment. Choose any sentence from your day-to-day interactions, and decide which operative words you wish to stress (or the syllables of the operative words you wish to stress). Sing all syllables of nonoperatives on the same pitch, emphasizing the operative words by singing up several notes or down several notes. (This is most effective when the pitch changes are at least a minor third apart.) The effect will be more akin to speak-singing. That is, elongate or stretch out your words beyond the point of what is considered to be natural for speaking. Let the vowels become much longer than they are in natural speech, and try to connect all sounds so that there are no stops except when necessary to breathe. It may sound as if you are chanting or entoning the words. Another option would be to utilize the text of any contemporary play, choosing a monologue that will provide a lot of variety in sentence structure.

It should be noted that the suggestion that the actor try entoning all words that are considered nonoperatives on the same pitch is made because this more clearly resembles the natural melodic choices of the speaking voice. That is, we speak more or less in a very tight pitch range (to be referred to as *neutral pitch* from here on), except on those words or syllables we wish to emphasize. Then we emphasize through pitch change and return to speaking in that narrow range. For example, in the sentence "I don't want to go to the store right now," one could choose to emphasize "want" and "store" by singing most of the phrase on one note and raising in pitch on these two words only. However, to explore pitch change further, when singing this exercise, it is not necessary to return to the neutral pitch range after each emphasized word. One could choose to stay on the pitch of the chosen operative word for a while, and then change pitch on the next operative word, and so on. Thus, one might sing "I don't" on one note, change to a higher pitch on "want," stay on that pitch for "to go to the," and sing a lower pitch on "store," remaining there for the rest of the phrase. In doing this, stay attuned to how pitch change affects emphasis.

Next, move on to the texts of the comedies. Again, any of the passages from Chapter 3 will suffice for this exercise, but you may wish to start with some shorter phrases, such as the list of similitudes found in the third exercise for working with similitudes. The following is an example of how one might sing a similitude as a recitative, noting which words will change pitch. Suggestions are also provided as to the nature of the pitch change.

Friendship without Freedom	"Friend"—a slight pitch inflection "ship" "without"—neutral pitch "Free"—slightly wider pitch inflection "dom"—neutral pitch
is as dull as Love without enjoyment	"is" "as"—neutral pitch "dull"—much lower pitch "as"—neutral pitch "Love"—wider pitch inflection "without" "en"—neutral pitch "joy"—slight pitch inflection "ment"—neutral pitch
or Wine without toasting	"or"—neutral pitch "Wine"—wider pitch inflection "without"—neutral pitch "toast"—slight pitch inflection "ing"—neutral pitch

Be sure to experiment with more complicated texts of dialogue, such as those containing lists, in order to experience ample opportunity for inflection and playing lower pitches as means to point certain words or syllables. Experiment further by holding a certain pitch longer (for more syllables), before changing to a new pitch to point an operative word, rather than returning to the neutral pitch. An example of this technique follows.

I won't be called names after I'm Married	"I" "won't" "be" "called"—first pitch "names"—higher pitch "after" "I'm"—same pitch "Mar"—even higher pitch "ied"—same as "after"
positively I won't be called Names	"positively" "I" "won't" "be" "called"—all on same lower pitch "Names"—slightly higher pitch
Ay as Wife, Spouse, My dear,	"Ay as"—same pitch "Wife" "Spouse"—slightly higher "My dear"—lower
Joy, Jewel, Love, Sweetheart	"Joy" "Jewel"—slightly higher "Love"—lower "Sweetheart"—lower still
and the rest of that Nauseous Cant	"and the rest of that"—aiming to re-create the starting pitch "Nauseous Cant"—much lower

RECITATIVE EXERCISE—PART II

The next step is to work with the material, still making pitch changes on chosen operative words, but to speak in a more naturalistic way. However, it is imperative not to bring the speech back to the more limited pitch range of contemporary everyday conversation. That is, now perform the text (or start with contemporary phrases), without singing or entoning, but maintain a clear sense of pitch change that is a bit wider than what is experienced in day-to-day exchanges. You may wish to start with the two examples analyzed in Part I, or use a passage in which you have already noted your pitch change choices. Again, any of the short passages from the preceding chapter provide ample opportunity for experimentation. In the process, try both marking the text beforehand as well as improvising. Try a bit of dialogue from the preceding chapter, and in addition to inflecting, try to find opportunities to lower your pitch, such as when wanting to undercut your partner with sarcasm, create unattractive imagery, or knock down your partner's previous line while engaging in bantering or other verbal warfare.

Tempo and Rhythm

To begin, it is important to understand the difference between these two terms. With respect to speech and music, understanding *tempo* seems simple enough. It refers to the pace of the speaking voice or music—how fast or slow one speaks or plays. *Rhythm* is a bit more complicated. It is helpful to think of note values when thinking of rhythm. Musical notes represent different fractional values or portions of time; they are units of time. Thus, it can be said that rhythm has to do with the ordering of time. With respect to the speaking voice, the speaker creates rhythm, or rhythmic variety, by creating different note values in sound. As a very simple demonstration, two words, each spelled with two letter *i*'s, have very different rhythms. The word *limit* is very short, each syllable moving very quickly through time. In the word *finite*, composed of two long *i*'s, each syllable takes longer to say. Additionally, in both words, the sound of the first syllable lasts longer than the sound of the second syllable. Thus, by the very nature of the varying durations of spoken syllables, it can be said that in executing the proper American English pronunciation of words, the voice cannot be without rhythm.

The actor, however, cannot get by on merely functional vocal rhythm. He needs to master the full potential of rhythmic variety inherent in the language of English dramatic literature; the same holds true for tempo. The following exercises will address rhythm as a method of pointing operative words, as well as a means to vocally create imagery and other literary devices. Experiments with tempo will address the pace of the texts, as well as the syntactical structures. All approaches to these vocal variables are designed to assist in creating the full musical potential of the speaking voice so that the highly adorned language of the comedies may be served.

Exercises for Tempo and Rhythm

TEMPO 1—WORDS, WORDS, WORDS!

One initial response to seventeenth-century comedy of manners is the recognition that there are so many words. This sheer amount of words, along with the need to create a sense of keeping the ball in play within any form of verbal battle, implies a quickness of tempo. The language must move forward quickly and, for the most part, lightly. However, it is imperative that the overall quick tempo is not achieved at the expense of good diction. All text must be intelligible. That is, sounds and syllables are not contracted beyond what is specifically noted in the texts; nor, for the most part, are they dropped altogether. Therefore, a good initial exercise is to utilize Laban's Flick or Dab when practicing lines at a comfortable clip. In musical terms, this tempo might be considered *allegretto*.

Work through the following passages, concentrating on the Flick and the Dab, while maintaining a quickness of tempo and clarity of speech. Challenge yourself by gradually accelerating your overall tempo on the repetition of one passage to test how quickly you can speak and maintain all the sounds of the words.

HORNER, FROM WYCHERLEY'S *COUNTRY WIFE*

'Tis as hard to be a good Fellow, a good Friend, and a Lover of Women, as 'tis to be a good Fellow, a good Friend, and a Lover of Money.

WITWOUD, FROM CONGREVE'S *WAY OF THE WORLD*

She hates Mirabell worse than a Quaker hates a parrot, or than a Fishmonger hates a hard Frost.

LYDIA, FROM WYCHERLEY'S *LOVE IN A WOOD*

He is like the desperate Banke-routes of this age, who if they can get people's fortunes into their hands, care not though they spend them in Goale, all their lives.

MANLY, FROM WYCHERLEY'S *PLAIN DEALER*

Thus Women, and Men like women, are too hard for us, when they think we do not hear 'em, and Reputation, like other Mistresses, is never true to a Man in his absence.

HORNER, FROM WYCHERLEY'S *COUNTRY WIFE*

There are Quacks in love, as well as Physick, who get but the fewer and worse Patients, for their boasting; a good name is seldom got by giving it ones self, and Women no more than honour are compass'd by bragging.

TEMPO 2—CREATING SYNTAX

Next, use the passages from the previous exercise, or any from Chapter 3, and experiment with achieving the overall clip of the speech while slowing down on the phrases you wish to emphasize. For example, in speaking the second passage noted in the previous exercise, it is quite clear that the speaker's primary intent is to create a similitude. Thus, much of the information in the sentence is already understood on the part of the listener. This information can move forward quite quickly, but the imagery of the two-part similitude may be spoken at a slower tempo. That is, all should move with a sense of allegretto, except for "Quaker hates a parrot" and "Fishmonger hates a hard Frost."

Now take a more complex passage between two characters and find all the deviations from the overall tempo that you may utilize to create meaning, to drive a point home, to undercut your partner, or to top your partner. Experiment with the following exchange between Millamant and Mirabell.

MIRABELL: Like Daphne she as lovely and as coy. Do you lock yourself up from me, to make my search more Curious? Or is this pretty Artifice contriv'd, to Signifie that here the Chase must end, and my pursuit be crown'ed, for you can fly no further.

MILLAMANT: Vanity! No I'll fly and be follow'd to the last moment, tho' I am upon the very Verge of Matrimony, I expect you shou'd solicite me as much as if I were wavering at the grate of a Monastery, with one foot over the threshold. I'll be solicited to the very last, nay and afterwards.

MIRABELL: What, after the last?

MILLAMANT: O, I should think I was poor and had nothing to bestow, if I were reduc'd to inglorious ease; and free'd from the Agreeable fatigues of solicitation.

MIRABELL: But do not you know, that when favours are conferr'd upon Instant and tedious Sollicitation, that they diminish in their value, and that both the giver Loses the grace, and the receiver lessens his Pleasure?

MILLAMANT: It may be in things of common Application; but never sure in Love.

RHYTHM 1—THE LONG AND THE SHORT NOTES

If speaking in an overall clip is desirable for this language, then one may construe that most of the note values are quite short. That is, the sound of most syllables does not last for a very long time. For instance, one might say that the predominant note values are *eighth notes* and *sixteenth notes*, musically speaking. Likewise, to emphasize certain words or syllables, one needs to stretch these sounds so that they occupy or move through more time. Thus, it could be said that the operative words or emphasized syllables are constructed on *quarter notes*, *half notes*, and perhaps some *whole notes* as well. It is this alternation between short sounds and long or stretched sounds that provides rhythmic interest to speech. Further, these rhythmic changes, like melodic changes, contribute to the creation of meaning. To understand these concepts more clearly, improvise on the following short sentences by choosing one syllable to stretch or elongate. Repeat the phrase, expanding a different syllable, noting how the meaning changes.

> Please, don't go right now.
> I don't want to see that movie.
> I am willing to do whatever it takes.
> I never said I wanted to go with you.

RHYTHM 2—LONG AND SHORT NOTES 2

Now practice this sense of long and short notes on the following passages. First, attempt a cold reading of the text, elongating the sounds that seem to call for emphasis. Next, mark your text, highlighting syllables within operative words as well as within specific imagery you wish to emphasize. Then perform the text, moving through the less important language on short notes and stretching the sounds you wish to stress through long notes, or elongation. An example is provided wherein all stretched syllables or words are noted. However, remember that all elongated words or syllables are not of equal time value. The relative importance of the word or syllable would determine the length of the stretch.

HORNER, FROM WYCHERLY'S COUNTRY WIFE

With your PARdon, ladies, I know, like GREAT MEN in OFFices, you seem to exact FLATtery and aTENDance ONLY from your FOLlowers, but you have reCEIVers about you, and such to pay, a man is aFRAID to pass your GRANTS; besides, we must let you WIN at CARDS, or we LOSE your HEARTS.

HEARTWELL, FROM CONGREVE'S OLD BATCHELOUR

Oh Manhood, where art thou! What am I come to? A Woman's Toy; at these years! Death, a bearded Baby for a Girl to dandle. O dotage, dotage! That ever that Noble passion, Lust, should ebb to this degree—no reflux of vigorous Blood; a Child—A meer Infant and would suck.

LADY WISHFORT, FROM CONGREVE'S WAY OF THE WORLD

O Sir Rowland, the hours that he has dy'd away at my feet, the Tears that he has shed, the Oaths that he has sworn, the Palpitations that he has felt, the Trances and the Tremblings, the Ardors and the Ecstacies the Kneelings and the Riseings, the Heart-Eyes! Oh no memory can Register.

CARELESS, FROM CONGREVE'S DOUBLE DEALER

Ah heavens, madam, you ruine me with Kindness; your Charming tongue pursues the Victory of your eyes, while at your Feet your poor Ardour dies . . . Ah why are you so Fair, so bewitching Fair? O let me grow to the ground here, and feast upon that hand; O let me press it to my heart, my aking trembling heart. The nimble movement shall instruct your Pulse, and teach to allarm Desire.

AMANDA, FROM VANBRUGH'S RELAPSE

Yet still 'tis safer to avoid the storm
The strongest vessels, if they put to sea,
May possibly be lost.
Wou'd I cou'd keep you here in this calm port for ever!
Forgive the weakness of a woman,
I am uneasy at your going to stay so long in town;

I know its false insinuating pleasures;
I know the force of its delusions;
I know the strength of its attacks;
I know the weak defence of nature;
I know you are a man—and I—a wife.

PUTTING IT ALL TOGETHER: EXPERIMENTING WITH PITCH, TEMPO, AND RHYTHM

When a speaker naturally emphasizes a word or phrase, she does not think about whether she is inflecting or if she is elongating a sound. Further, chances are that she may be using more than one variable in highlighting a word or phrase. For the actor, however, the vocal variables are the palette of colors, strokes, or textures with which she paints with her voice. Thus, these artistic vocal choices are often chosen consciously, perhaps more so in the performance of period style plays than in modern realism. It then behooves a beginning actor to go through the steps of making these conscious choices by marking text to highlight the operative words, colorful imagery, and syntactical considerations.

Exercise

At this point, it is beneficial to take any of the text on which you have previously worked and mark all the important words, imagery, and any syntactical concerns, such as the balance of a similitude. Then improvise with pitch, rhythm, and tempo changes to highlight these and create meaning. Try many different versions, first focusing on keeping the variables separate and distinct. Next, do not be concerned with separating the variables out. That is, you may inflect in pitch and stretch a note value at the same time, or concurrently slow down and lower the pitch of an entire phrase. It is helpful to stay attuned to what is happening in your voice; that is, be sensitive to the changes in the vocal variables, especially when using more than one concurrently.

PLAYING THE SOUNDS

As discussed in the section on tempo, the clip, or the light, quick nature of the speed of the language, cannot be achieved at the expense of good diction. The sounds of the language must be fully played in order to appreciate the sense of adornment and the artificiality of the manners of the society portrayed in the comedies. The consonants, whether plosives, sibilants, or fricatives, must be tasted and relished. The vowels, particularly in operative words, may be entoned or nearly sung. As this is not a textbook specifically for voice and diction, this unit simply provides exercises to help enhance an awareness of playing the sounds of the vowels and consonants to assist in the creation of vocally lively text. Further, the unit does not endeavor to engage in a thorough study of the classification and formation of the various phonemes.

Exercises

Working with Vowels

COMMUNICATING WITH THE VOWELS

As a warm-up to the following exercise, engage in conversation with a partner utilizing only vowel sounds. It may be helpful to choose a topic beforehand and then chat, argue, disagree, gossip, or tell a story utilizing only the vowel sounds of the words you speak. Let these sounds run together within a syntactical phrase. Become very aware of emphasis, the length of vowels, and the color or timbre of the sounds you emit.

ENTONING THE VOWELS

This exercise assists the actor in becoming aware of how the vowels create the sense of flow or ongoing melody in speech. Choose any short passage to start, and entone the vowel sounds only. Keep the voice smooth and connected, changing pitch when you feel compelled to. Play no consonant sounds at all! For example, look at the phrase "Damn'd Money! It's Master's potent rival still; and, like a saucy pimp, corrupts it self, the Mistress it procures for us." The vowels that need to be sustained in order to flow into the subsequent ones would be played as follows:

Damn'd Money	short *a* to the short *u* to the long *e*
It's Master's potent	short *i* to short *a* to long *o* to short *e*
rival still	to long *i* to short *i*
and, like a saucy pimp	short *a* to long *i* to short *u* to *aw* sound to long *e* to short *i*
corrupts it self	*aw* sound to short *u* to short *i* to short *e*
the Mistress it	short *u* to short *i* to short *e* to short *i*
procures for us	long *o* to long *oo* to *aw* sound to short *u*

All of these vowels should flow one right into the next, except when necessary to breathe. Do not worry too much about sustaining the phonetically correct vowel sound; rather, the intent should be the sense of getting the most out of sustaining vowels with respect to pitch and flow. Try this exercise on several passages, sensing also the different points of resonance in the body for the different vowels. That is, where do the different vowels seem to live? Feel the long *e* buzz in the front of the face; experience the *aw* resonate in the mouth and also the chest; find the tingling of the short *a* in the upper cheek bones. Enjoy each of the sensations the vowels produce.

Working with Consonants

SENSING THE CONSONANTS—SILLY ALLITERATIVE PHRASES

Since the inner man of the age was judged by the outer social mask, it follows that clarity of speech was a goal for which to strive. Further, since the fops in the comedies represent those people in society who took social practices to extremes, the consonants can be very valuable tools in the creation of these characters. Thus, this exercise functions to assist the actor in sensing and playing the full capabilities of the consonant phonemes. The true man of quality can support his proper social mask through clarity of speech, and the fop may be portrayed by his penchant for overplaying the consonants.

Devise any silly or nonsensical alliterative phrase that utilizes similar consonant sounds. That is, one can be improvised around any sibilant sounds, not just the sound of *s*. Therefore, one could write a phrase using *s*, *z*, and *sh*, such as "Silly Sands should salivate zestfully when shining on a searing desert." Further, one could devise a phrase around cognates, or pairs of voiced and unvoiced consonants, such as *p* and *b*, *d* and *t*, *v* and *f*, and so on. Play with as many different combinations as possible, being as precise as you can. Next perform a second version of your phrase, in which the consonants seem to be overplayed or overdone.

SENSING THE CONSONANTS IN TEXT

Next, move on to short pieces of text, such as from the lists of similitudes and epigrams in the previous chapter. Read several passages aloud, staying highly sensitive to the sensation of the consonants. Sense the explosion of the *p* and *b* on the lips, for example. Feel the tingle of the buzz of the *z* on the upper gum ridge. Let the *t* and *d* explode off the tip of the tongue and the gum ridge. Next, overdo the production of many consonants, particularly on words you wish to emphasize. Imagine a person who takes great pride in his precision and clarity of speech. Flaunt the sounds as you would a new outfit or hairdo, particularly whichever sounds tend to be your favorites. For example, consider the following passage spoken by Witwoud in *The Way of the World* and a possible foppish rendering for practice.

Thou hast uttered Volumes, Folios
In less than DeCimo Sexto, my
Dear LaCedomonian
Sirrah PeTulanT thou arT an
EPitomizer of worDS.

overplay the fricatives V and F
push the sibilant S

spit out the plosives of P
and T and overtly buzz the
frontal DZ

PUTTING IT ALL TOGETHER—SOUND BATTLES

With a partner, choose any short two-person scene previously cited or one of your own. Engage in vocal warfare, trying to outdo, put down, and simply outsound your partner. First work merely with the vowel sounds contained in your lines. Next, focus exclusively on the consonants. It is not imperative that you identify and play all the vowels or all consonants. Rather, try to glean the main ones utilized within a phrase and play these. Elongate the vowels and let them connect together. Explode, buzz, and/or sense the consonants, as they become the weaponry with which you do battle. Then, mix up the vowel and consonant sounds, playing one or the other as it seems appropriate at any given moment. Finally, speak the actual texts (still improvising with the idea of doing vocal battle with all the vowels and consonants), staying sensitized to the elongated vowel sounds and the precision of the consonants.

SCENE ANALYSIS

Utilizing a portion of the same passage analyzed at the end of the previous chapters, suggestions will be made for vocal choices. For the purposes of this analysis, each sentence will not be analyzed in its entirety according to all the topics of this chapter. Rather, several suggestions will be made concerning operative words, Laban technique, pitch, rhythm, tempo, and clarity in the sounds of the speech for each passage as a whole, taking into account the analysis of language and the devices of wit that was previously performed.

Mirabell, Witwoud, Millamant, Mrs. Fainall, and Mincing from Congreve's *Way of the World*

MIRABELL: You seem to be unattended, Madam—You us'd to have the Beau-mond Throng after you; and a Flock of gay fine Perrukes hovering round you.
[Stretch "unattended," with an inflection on the third syllable, as this is Mirabell's first sarcastic remark to Millamant. Stretch and lower pitch on

"Beau-mond" to create the image. Flick the word "Flock" in order to play that strong final k. Float the image of "gay fine Perrukes"—again flicking the final k—and stretch and inflect the first syllable of "hovering" to play this important operative word.]

WITWOUD: Like Moths about a Candle—I had like to have lost my Comparison for want of breath.
[Dab the image of the similitude, inflecting "moths" and "candle" as operative words to relish the fop's wit. Change to wringing in the second half of the line to suggest Witwoud's being "out of breath," feasibly having to run to keep up with Millamant.]

MILLAMANT: O I have deny'd my self Airs to Day. I have walk'd as fast through the Crowd—
[Glide effortlessly through the first sentence. Stretch "O" on a slightly lower than neutral pitch and stretch "deny'd." Elongate especially "Airs" to suggest the double entendre of her usage. Experience the lightness of the stretched vowel in "Airs." Pick up the tempo in the next sentence, paying particular attention to the first half of the similitude to be created by inflecting and playing the wonderful consonants on "crowd"—the main operative word.]

WITWOUD: As a Favourite in disgrace; and with as few Followers.
[Quickly jump in to cut off Millamant, inflecting "Favourite," but lowering pitch into "in disgrace" to play this antithesis. Dab the remainder of the similitude, relishing the feel of the fs.]

MILLAMANT: Dear Mr. Witwoud, truce with your Similitudes; For I am as sick of 'em—
[Glide effortlessly through this expression of your disdain, on a low pitch for "Dear Mr. Witwoud," beautifully inflecting on "truce" and "Similitudes." Set off the operative word "sick" by flicking, using a shorter note value and inflecting.]

WITWOUD: As a Phisician of a good air—I cannot help it Madam, tho' 'tis against myself.
[Again, quickly jump in and cut off Millamant. Really stretch and inflect "Phisician," relishing the sibilants and the fricative f. Inflect "air," as well. Speed up and undercut yourself on the entire next phrase, clearly relishing your own facility in wit.]

MILLAMANT: Yet again! Mincing, stand between me and his wit.
[Let out the irritation by speaking all short notes and in a somewhat high range on "Yet again!" Regain control or demonstrate your fatigue by gliding the rest of the phrase, emphasizing "me" and "wit" with slight inflections.]

WITWOUD: Do Mrs. Mincing, like a Skreen before a great Fire. I confess I do blaze to Day, I am too bright.

[Jump right in with an elongated and inflected "Do," and play up yet another similitude by stretching "Skreen" and "great Fire." Speed up the next phrase with shorter notes, yet stretch "blaze" and "bright" to really relish your play on words. Enjoy the long a and the long i sounds. Punch the bs on both words.]

MRS. FAINALL: But dear Millamant, why were you so long?
[Quickly jump into the fray to cut off Witwoud, speaking the first half of the sentence on short notes. Float the second half to mask any irritation, stretching "why" and "long" as operative words.]

MILLAMANT: Long! Lord, have I not made violent haste? I have ask'd every living thing I met for you; I have enquir'd after you, as after a new Fashion.
[Slash the exclamation of "Long," and to a lesser extent, "Lord." Stretch and inflect "violent haste." Float through the next phrase and then play the operative words. Balance the similitude aurally by inflecting the second syllable of "enquir'd" and stretching or gliding "you" and "Fashion."]

WITWOUD: Madam, truce with your Similitudes—No, you met her Husband and did not ask him for her.
[Display a lack of true social grace by undercutting Millamant and throwing her own words back at her. Speak a bit lower than normal and stretch "truce" and especially "your." Disagree with her and scold her a bit by dabbing the next line and stretching "Husband" and "him" as operative words.]

MILLAMANT: By your leave Witwoud, that were like enquiring after an old Fashion, to ask a Husband for his Wife.
[With effortless ease, glide into the quick retort to skillfully return the volley. Play up the similitude and the antithesis created with "old Fashion" by stretching it and lowering the pitch. Play the operative words "Husband" by stretching the first syllable and slightly inflecting and "Wife" by slightly stretching and lowering pitch.]

WITWOUD: Hum, a hit, a hit, a palpable hit, I confess it.
[Elongate "Hum," and then flick the middle section, playing the ts, ps, and bs. Glide into the admission of your defeat.]

MRS. FAINALL: You were dress'd before I came abroad.
[So as not to let Millamant off the hook, quickly get back into the game, by undercutting Witwoud, lowering the pitch but masking with a Glide. Emphasize "dress'd," "before," and "abroad" with slight stretches.]

MILLAMANT: Ay, that's true—O but then I had—Mincing what had I? Why was I so long?
[Refuse to indulge in any sincerity, by floating the first two short phrases, changing pitch but staying in a relatively high range. Dab the other two short

phrases, relinquishing any responsibility, and inflect and float the last word beautifully.]

MINCING: O Mem, your Laship staid to peruse a Pecquet of Letters.
[Buying into the game, flick off the answer, thereby also highlighting Mincing's somewhat strange pronunciations.]

MILLAMANT: O ay, Letters—I had Letters—I am persecuted with Letters—I hate Letters—No Body knows how to write Letters; and yet one has 'em, one does not know why—They serve one to pin up one's Hair.
[Enjoy the dissembling by floating a quickly returned response. Seize the opportunity to turn the subject to railing against letters, by hitting the word "letters" harder and harder each time it is said. Let it begin as a Press and change to a Punch. Skillfully dab the final sentence, returning to a higher range to indicate a lack of sincerity.]

WITWOUD: Is that the Way? Pray madam, do you pin up your Hair with all your Letters? I find I must keep Copies.
[Taking her response as truth, wring the first question, stretching "that" and "Way." Flick the second question, enjoying and overplaying the ps and ts. Slash or wring the final sentence, but in a somewhat higher pitch range to attempt masking.]

MILLAMANT: Only with those in Verse, Mr. Witwoud. I never pin up my Hair with Prose. I Fancy ones Hair wou'd not curl if it were pinn'd up with Prose. I think I try'd once Mincing.
[Enjoy the witty response by stretching the first sentence and undercutting Witwoud with a lower pitch. Go further with this by stretching "never," "Hair," and "Prose" in the next sentence, particularly the long o of "Prose." Dab the following witty, ambiguous pronouncement, stretching "curl," and play the ps very clearly. Shrug it all off, flicking the final short sentence.]

MINCING: O Mem, I shall never forget it.
[Enjoy the mock seriousness of the situation by lowering and stretching this phrase.]

MILLAMANT: Ay, poor Mincing tift and tift all morning.
[Flick out the insincerity of this statement.]

MINCING: Till I had the Cremp in my Fingers I'll vow Mem. And all to no purpose. But when your Laship pins it up with Poetry, it sits so pleasant the next Day as any Thing, and is so pure and crips.
[Wring the first two sentences and stretch "Cremp" and "Fingers," furthering the mock seriousness of the situation. Dab the remaining lines in a slightly higher pitch range, playing all the ps, ds and ts.]

WITWOUD: Indeed, so crips?
[Lower pitch on "Indeed so," then raise it noticeably and really play the consonants on "crips" to make fun of Mincing's manner of speaking.]

MINCING: You're such a Critick, Mr. Witwoud.
[Lower the pitch and play the ks and t of "Critick."]

MILLAMANT: Mirabell, did not you take Exceptions last Night?—O ay, and went away—Now I think on't I'm angry—No now I think on't I'm pleased—For I believe I gave you some Pain.
[Seize control of the conversation, by gliding in to focus on Mirabell, with a slight sense of wring on "Exceptions last Night?" and on "O ay, and went away," raising the pitch. Slightly slash the next phrase, and change your mind to maintain the upper hand, by floating, "No now I think on't I'm pleased." Set off "Pain" by stretching the long a and playing the p.]

MIRABELL: Do's that please you?
[Don't betray any hurt feelings, by floating the question and using a moderately high pitch.]

MILLAMANT: Infinitely; I love to give Pain.
[Float and stretch "Infinitely." Lower the pitch on the next phrase, stretching "love."]

NOTES

1. Joan Wildeblood, *The Polite World: A Guide to English Manners and Deportment* (London: Davis-Poynter, 1973), p. 92.
2. Jean Newlove, *Laban for Actors and Dancers* (New York: Routledge, 1993).
3. *The New Harvard Dictionary of Music*, Don Michael Randal, ed. (Cambridge: Belknap Press of Harvard University Press, 1986), p. 638.
4. In her wonderful *Freeing Shakespeare's Voice*, Kristen Linklater provides an excellent warm-up that allows the performer to experience the resonance, pitch, energy, and moods of specific sounds. Because the exercise progresses through the lowest (in the body) to the highest resonators, it provides an effective warm-up for pitch. See Chapter 1 of her text for a thorough delineation. Kristin Linklater, *Freeing Shakespeare's Voice* (New York: Theatre Communications, 1992).
5. *The New Harvard Dictionary of Music*, p. 682.

5

THE PHYSICAL LIVES
OF CHARACTERS
Movement, Fashion, and the Details
of Deportment

INTRODUCTION

As noted in Chapter 1, with the restoration of the monarchy, many of the practices, behaviors, and manners from the French court were transplanted to English society. This cannot be attributed purely to Charles II and the years he spent in Paris, for the era of the Restoration was truly the age of France. France set the rules of fashion, literature, and manners for the rest of Europe, and all things French flowed freely into England. Freed from the yoke of Puritanism, the British upper classes hungrily sought out the fineries and luxuries so vigorously denied them during the Commonwealth. Everything from such amenities as fine fabrics and gastronomical delicacies to courtly manners were ardently pursued and more readily available. And although King Charles was noted for and prided himself on a new ease of courtly deportment, the seemingly never-ending flow of the predominantly French manners created a highly complex, highly artificial code of deportment and manners. The verbal components of this code of behavior have already been discussed in Chapter 3, with respect to the honing of language into an art form. However, this complexity was most clearly manifested in the physical lives or deportment of the fashionable set. Since the quality of a person and one's inner character was measured by his or her outer bearing, well-defined social mandates governed movement, posture, carriage, and gestures, all of which were carefully honed by tutors and dancing masters. To be an accepted member of this set, one was required to be accomplished in the myriad of details associated with the likes of bowing and curtsying, snuff taking, strolling, greeting friends and persons of higher rank, using a fan, holding one's lace cuffs "just so," and removing and replacing one's hat. Additionally, all of these details of decorum were to be carried off with elegance and ease; and although one studied these carefully prescribed manners from the time of childhood, the physical execution of such was to appear unstudied. That is, all the details of this highly artificial code of physical behavior was to be executed with effortless ease and must appear to be natural, as opposed to learned behavior. To this end, not only were dancing masters employed from the time of youth, but countless etiquette books and rules for civility proliferated, defining seemingly every nuance of human interrelationship. These guides to deportment—indispensable to the gentlemen and ladies of Restoration England—leave a clear set of guidelines for the social behaviors reflected and parodied in the comedies and, thus, are invaluable resources for contemporary performance.[1]

For the contemporary actor, achieving an appearance of effortless ease in attempting to re-create such a wide range of prescribed physical behavior is a daunting task. It is particularly so when one may have only four to six weeks to learn a precise physical code that was originally learned and polished over a lifetime. However, through concerted practice in rehearsal or workshop, the basic components of this mode of physical communication are achievable. Further, for actors who study dance, facility in this movement is readily attainable. On the other hand, as previously discussed, the larger stumbling block is usually that of a misalignment of thinking, by which the actor views the numerous articles of decorum as inauthentic behavior or something to be layered on top of one's communication or one's acting. It must be remembered that within this polite set, "the manners were the man." The arduously created mask of manners represented the "true" Restoration gentleman and lady. And as Athene Seyler noted in her wonderful *Craft of Comedy*, "in artificial comedy the chief concern of playwright and actor is the external manners of a given period which, though superficial, yet deeply affect behavior; and from these the comedy springs."[2] Thus, for the actor to realign his thinking, these *externals* must take on primary significance. Further, the highly refined social mask that was presented to the world by Restoration gallants and ladies must be viewed as a necessary component of nonverbal communication. From a seventeenth-century perspective, an artifice-laden physical life not only was reflective of one's inner life but represented the means by which one expressed oneself and communicated nonverbally. By adapting this line of thinking, the correct use and execution of a bow or the turnout of the legs, for instance, is not performed as a hollow mechanical act. One's social status was judged by these acts and postures. When portraying a Mirabell, a Mellefont, or a Ranger, one must clearly embrace the sensibility that, to a large extent, these characters created and maintained their social standing by communicating physically that they were cultured, graceful, and, thus, authentic denizens of their world. Likewise, when preparing a Millamant or a Cynthia, the various positions and placements of the fan cannot be viewed as empty gestures to be thoughtlessly aped. Rather, the *language of the fan* represents a whole array of meaningful, nonverbal gestures by which a myriad of messages may be communicated. Further, a lady also communicated her social standing in part through her facility with this nonverbal language. Finally, as suggested by Seyler, it was these externals with which the playwrights were fascinated and that lay at the core of the comedy.

THE MASK OF FASHION

Before delving into any movement work and the specifics of the Restoration's physical mask, a basic understanding of the costume or fashion of the period is necessary. Not only will it be helpful to achieve a clear picture of the mask of fashion in order to complete the picture of the mask of the polite world, it is also necessary to understand how the fashion of the period restricted, informed, or even defined the movement and gesture of the human body. A basic understanding of the fashion dictates of the era, therefore, will enhance the progress of the movement work to follow in this chapter.

Just as the manners, deportment, and speech of the ladies and gallants reveal a high degree of complexity of artifice, the fashion of the period is also reflective of this overall sensibility. Lucy Barton, in her *Historic Costume for the Stage*, notes, "Curls, ribbons, puffs, flounces, and feathers appeared wherever they could find clinging-space."[3] A sense of adornment and a careful structuring of the human form completed the carefully constructed social mask. It was a time of peacock excess for both men and women, and the clothes "were the person." In other words, to be a proper member of the polite world began with the display of sumptuous clothing worn well. The inner person was not judged solely by the ability to turn a phrase or turn a calf, but also by the cut and style of, and deportment in using, one's clothing.

Since the comedies were a reflection of the behaviors and practices of the polite world, this necessity to wear beautiful, fashionable clothing well was mirrored many times over. Lyn Oxenford, in her *Playing Period Plays*, notes, "Clothes and lovemaking seem to the actor to dominate all these plays."[4] In *Man of Mode*, the entire first scene (which is quite lengthy) occurs in Dorimant's rooms, where he is dressing for the day. As he converses with the orange woman, the shoemaker, a footman, young Bellair, and Medley, his man fusses about him, dressing him and arranging his accessories. Truly this is one of the most self-conscious tributes to the polite set. Additionally, in the same play, one of the most outrageous slaves—and perhaps the quintessential slave—to all things fashionable (particularly clothing), is Sir George Etherege's masterpiece of character, Sir Fopling Flutter. Through this character, Etherege reflects contemporary society's penchant for mocking the man who strives too hard to remain in step with fashion. Indeed, the man who behaved thus was frowned upon by true gentlemen and ladies and was the source of much laughter in the theatre.

Men's Fashion

Starting with the feet and moving up, until the late seventeenth century, men wore square-toed shoes with long tongues and open sides. Just before the turn of the century, the sides were not open. Throughout the period of the Restoration, heels ranged from low, thick ones to slimmer, high ones. The red heel remained in fashion throughout. Shoe roses were in fashion early on but were soon replaced with ribbons, which were often wired to stand out.

Full tubular breeches were worn at first, but then *petticoat breeches* (very full, often decorative breeches that sometimes were cut more as a divided skirt) became the height of fashion. Later in the era, slimmer breeches (more like knickers) became popular among the polite set. Silk stockings with decorative tops were worn on the legs and sometimes were pulled up over the lower edge of the breeches.

Over the torso, layering started with the full shirt or *jerkin*, both the body and the sleeves of which were very full and gathered. The shirt, nearly always white, opened in the front and closed at the neck with a drawn string. The neckline could be folded over almost into a collar and could support a cravat. Early on, men wore a stiff collar band, but they soon favored the more elegant cravat, which was a long cloth with laced ends that was wrapped around the neck and tied snuggly at the throat. Eventually, cravats became more elaborated with a stiffened, lace-edged bow at the throat. Wristbands were sewn with ruffles and were often long enough to fall over the wearer's hand. Early in the period, waistcoats were sometimes not worn over the shirt but grew in popularity as the era progressed. They started out short and then progressively lengthened until they were almost as long as the coat itself. The coat, which was worn long (often reaching to the knees) and loosely shaped to the body, was heavy with huge, elaborate cuffs. At first, coats were collarless and sometimes had a skirted look about them. As the era ensued, the coats became slimmer and somewhat more formfitting. The coat was quite heavy, usually made of heavy brocade with elaborate embroidery of silver and gold thread. Pockets were low and large. When weather necessitated, full capes of about knee length were worn over the coats.

Hair was worn long, with a proliferation of curls falling loosely about the shoulders. Wigs were required to supply the necessary fashionable fullness of curls, eventually reaching monumental proportions and sometimes standing up in two points or dividing into three individual tufts. Atop the wigs, large plumed hats were worn. As the wigs grew in fullness, hats were either not worn, but carried, or not removed so as to maintain one's coiffure.

Accessories for men proliferated during the period, providing the modern actor with a wide array of gestural capabilities. Swords were worn at the side until well after the turn of the century, when Beau Brummel (important arbiter of fashion) dictated that the wearing of swords was no longer fashionable. Walking sticks were carried, along with large wig combs, pomanders at the waist, and elegant laced gloves. Watches hung from the neck or were worn inside the waistcoat. Additionally, men, like women, wore makeup and applied patches to cover pox marks and blemishes, as well as for decoration. Finally, large square or round muffs were carried for the hands along with the ever-useful large laced handkerchief.

Note that the costume design for Mirabell in The Way of the World (Figure 5–1) reveals many aspects of the gentleman's fashion around the year 1700. Mirabell sports a long coat with elaborate cuffs, a full-sleeved shirt—as indicated by the gathered cuffs—the long waistcoat that suggests fine fabric, a full head of loose curls, the plumed hat, the thick-heeled, long-tongued shoes, the twisted cravat, and slimmed-down breeches. Notice that he carries his sword, hanging off to his left side, and also carries a walking stick.

In Figure 5–2, Petulant (a false wit in The Way of the World) wears a full-skirted coat, which also displays the oversized cuffs. The right shoulder of his coat is decorated with a cluster of ribbons. Over his coat he wears a muff and a small bag. Note the length of the wrist ruffles on his shirt. His cravat has been tied into a bow, and he is wearing padded hose to enhance the shape of his calves. His wig is much larger and fuller than Mirabell's and is also built up into two small peaks at the crown of the head. His shoes, which have very long tongues, are adorned with bows. He wears several rings; makeup is implied; and he also wears a face patch. He displays a lace-trimmed handkerchief. Also notice that there are several plumes on his hat.

FIGURE 5–1 Costume Design for Mirabell, *Way of the World*
ⓒ 2001 by Jeanette de Jong

FIGURE 5–2 Costume Design for Petulant, *Way of the World*
© 2001 by Jeanette de Jong

Figure 5–3, a costume design for Sir Fopling Flutter in *Man of Mode*, suggests a strong French influence and the extremes to which a fop might venture in fashion. Sir Fopling wears a lavish, full-bottomed wig, upon which a hat with multitudinous feathers perches. His jacket is short, as are its sleeves, revealing many layers of gathered shirtsleeves. Notice that

FIGURE 5–3 Costume Design for Sir Fopling Flutter, *Man of Mode*
© 2001 by Jeanette de Jong

bows of ribbon cling to any available space. His sword hangs from an elaborate sash about his shoulder, and he sports elaborate gloves, which he flaunts in the play. His breeches are of particular interest as they are extraordinarily full-skirted petticoat breeches. His overall look is that of an overly adorned wedding cake. The designer has drawn from several different decades to fashion this whimsical, somewhat outrageous, design.

Women's Fashion

Beginning with the feet, women also wore low heels. As the feet were usually not seen (except for the tips when seated), women's shoes were not as elaborately decorated as those of the men. Mules were popular, especially indoors, and shoes were made of leather, silk, satin, and brocades. Inside the shoes, ladies wore stockings that were gartered just above or just below the knee.

Over a loose-fitting shift or chemise (usually made of linen), women wore highly decorated petticoats, which were often exposed when skirts were gathered up for walking outdoors. Under this petticoat, a hoop or panniers might also be worn, which increased the fullness of the skirt. This fullness, however, did not reach the great expanse that was fashionable in the Georgian era. Skirts for polite ladies were full and bell-shaped and reached to the floor. When simple skirts were pulled back, the underskirts were slightly shorter and made walking easier. As the period progressed, methods for pulling back the skirts became more and more elaborated, often requiring stays or ribbons hanging from the shoulders. Trains were often worn both indoors and out, indoor wear allowing for shorter ones. Further, short decorative aprons were often added over the outer skirt. Skirts and gowns were typically made of brocades or satins and were heavily trimmed with lace.

The bodice was well stiffened with stays of wood or bone lining the front and the back of the corsets. These bones kept the spine erect and had the added effect of aiding the display of the décolletage. In approximately the first twenty years of the period, both the front and the back of the bodice were pointed and long, but these shortened later in the era. Outer bodices were typically made of the same fabric as the outer skirt. Early in the period, the arms were kept open to display the pretty white sleeves of a chemise, which were tied up around the elbow. Around the 1690s, sleeves were attached and arrived at the popular elbow length. Throughout the period, bodices were low-cut, even when the chemise was visible at the chest. Pretty kerchiefs were often worn to cover this area. Capes, often with attached *capuchons* (large hoods), and large shawls were typical outerwear.

At the beginning of the period, a more natural look in women's hair was in vogue, with curls clustering at the back and soft loose ones lying delicately around the face. Curls were sometimes wired to stay away from the face, and ribbons were woven into the hair. Before the turn of the century, hairdos became more formal, with the front of the hair waved and built up and away from the forehead. This look was completed with the stiffened lace *fontange*, which was worn high over the forehead.

Accessories also proliferated for the lady. The fan was her indispensable tool for communication and a weapon for verbal warfare. Pomanders were worn about the waist; masks were carried for walking outdoors, as were muffs, canes, and tiny silk parasols. The lady often bejeweled herself with rings that were worn on every finger, as well as with necklaces, bracelets, and jeweled bows. A watch and a small elegant box for comfits were also carried.

In the third costume design for *The Way of the World* (Figure 5–4), Millamant is revealing her shorter underskirt, as the more elaborate overskirt is tied back with ribbons. The skirt, aided by panniers, falls into the typical bell shape. A train is suggested. The torso is clearly stiffened by corsetry and the bodice is cut somewhat long. Note the elaborate line of bows that adorns the bodice. The chemise is visible, as is evidenced by the short row of lace at the top of the bodice. Millamant's sleeves end at the popular elbow length and are adorned with gathered ruffs, lace, and bows. Her hair is fashioned into loose, more natural curls, and she dons the typical fontange. She has chosen a somewhat conservative necklace and carries the necessary fan.

Figure 5–5 (a costume design for Melantha in *Marriage a la Mode*) reveals how a woman obsessed with fashion might dress in a period about thirty years prior to the period suggested by Millamant's costume. Her outer skirt, like that of Millamant, is also tied back, revealing an even more elaborate underskirt than that designed for Millamant. The skirt is constructed in tiers, creating a wedding cake effect. These tiers, combined with larger panniers, create a more pronounced bell shape. Notice the two layers of tassels and the lace at the hemline. The dress obviously has an attached train. Her bodice is also clearly stiffened with corsetry, and although the dress sleeves end at the elbow, the sleeves of her chemise are quite long and have several layers of ruffle. Her hair is fashioned in more structured curls, and she dons a very elaborate fontange, which consists of three layers. She wears more jewelry than Millamant and holds a fan and a muff. Note the small mask hanging from her waist and her generous application of makeup and patches.

FIGURE 5–4 Costume Design for Millamant, *Way of the World*
© 2001 by Jeanette de Jong

FIGURE 5-5 Costume Design for Melantha, *Marriage a la Mode*
© 2001 by Jeanette de Jong

A CONSIDERATION OF REHEARSAL COSTUMES

Because the fashion of the day has a keen influence on the movement dictates in portraying these Restoration characters, it is strongly suggested that rehearsal costumes are used to approximate the fashion when performing the exercises in this chapter. This is particularly important when learning the details of movement, such as the walk, the bows, and the curtsies. The following is a list of suggestions for instances in which more authentic rehearsal costumes are not available.

For Men

Feet

Use leather shoes or dress boots with heels of at least three-quarters inch in height.

Legs

If rehearsal breeches are not available, to achieve a sense of petticoat breeches or early period breeches in general, old slacks cut off just at the knee work well. For breeches of the later part of the period, sweatpants or exercise pants pushed up to the knee will suffice. Dress slacks will also service if they are tied up just below the knee with a scarf, for instance. Jeans are not appropriate. It is advisable to also have a collection of knee socks or tights for men to wear with the breeches.

Torsos

Start with any gathered or loose-fitting shirt. A general "peasant" shirt will do. When none are available, modern men's dress shirts will suffice, particularly when they are oversized. It is extremely helpful to stitch lace or a gathered strip of fabric to the cuffs of the shirts. Vests are important; and for later in the era, the longer, the better. However, an assortment of modern men's vests that can be buttoned will provide the sense of layering and stiffening of the torso. With respect to coats, it is ideal if ones of the appropriate length can be found. Contemporary men's (and even women's) overcoats and raincoats will provide the necessary thigh or knee length of the Restoration coat. To achieve fullness at the bottom of the coat, the side seams may be opened from just below the waist to the bottom hem. It is also helpful if the coats are slightly oversized for the individual, so that cuffs can be slightly opened up at the wrist seams, and then turned back up to the elbow. If longer coats are not available, contemporary blazers or suit jackets will achieve not only the layered sense but also a feeling of formality.

Heads

If a collection of wigs is available, it is helpful for the actors to work with them. It is very important that the men work with hats. A wide variety of styles will function well for the hat work, including most any wide-brimmed hat, women's summer sun hats, or even straw hats. Caps of any type are inappropriate.

Accessories

A collection of women's scarves of various sizes is strongly advised. Men may wrap the longer ones around the neck to function as cravats. Further, if a bit of lace is sewn to the ends of these scarves, more elaborate cravats may be created. Smaller or square scarves will serve as handkerchiefs. Walking sticks or canes are also helpful, and may double as swords if belts are also provided in which to carry them. Gloves are also good to work with; some work gloves constructed of softer fabrics will suggest the more elaborate cuffs. Finally, to approximate snuff boxes, small women's compacts work well, as does any small ornamental box that may be carried in a pocket. The presently popular small, hinged mint boxes are also excellent. However, the ideal facsimile is a small spring-actioned box.

For Women

Feet

It is imperative that women work in shoes with small heels of about one-half to two inches. These should be dress shoes, not platform shoes or other thick-soled shoes. The heel must be defined as separate from the remainder of the sole of the shoe. *Character* shoes are always good.

Lower Body

Women must work in long, floor-length, gathered skirts. Ideally, these skirts should be worn over petticoats; if not available, several skirts may be worn one atop another; aprons will also suffice.

Torso

Perhaps the most difficult component to work with if rehearsal costumes are not available is the stiffening of the female torso. Because the shape and structure of corsets and stiffened bodices differed widely over the ages, for the movement work, precise historical accuracy is not necessary. What is important, however, is that the female torso be stiffened from either the navel or the waist up to the chest just under the armpits. Even though the exact line of the torso, and thus the precise area of the torso that is stiffened, will not be completely accurate, a variety of period corsets will suffice, as will much female support underwear that is available today. However, if modern underwear is used, that which is stiffened with boning is preferable. Through the support and stiffening supplied by these, the actor may, at the very least, experience the constriction of the torso and the restriction of movement. Over or under these corsets, the same type of peasant shirt as suggested for the men may be used. However, sleeves should end at or just below the elbow.

Accessories

The one essential accessory, or personal prop, is the fan. These should be pleated, folding fans of about eight to eighteen inches in length. It is very helpful if ribbon or string can be tied to the base of the fan so that the actor may wear it around her wrist. Nonessential accessories include a full or half-mask, small ornaments or boxes approximating pomanders to be worn about the waist, muffs, handkerchiefs, and walking sticks.

FASHION AND MOVEMENT: A BRIEF CONSIDERATION OF SPACE

Finally, before the movement work commences, it will be helpful to have a cursory understanding of spatial considerations affecting the socially prescribed movement of the day. Not only was the dress of Restoration gentlemen and ladies far more flamboyant than modern everyday garb, but the mere space taken up, particularly by the women's dress, was more extensive than that by modern clothing. Further, as mentioned, the sense of displaying one's clothing was a social imperative; and in order to effect this display, open or empty space is required. That is, the arrangement of furniture typical to the average modern middle-class home would severely encumber the movement required for the display of seventeenth-century women's fashion, not to mention the actors' functional movement alone. During the Restoration, interior decors were arranged formally with this idea of open space in mind. Furniture did not cluster together so as to encumber movement. Pathways to chairs, settees, and benches were kept clear. Even outdoors, the formally designed gardens and walkways allowed for the freedom of movement and a sense of display.

Additionally, the physical execution of manners (to be delineated later) also required a sense of open space. Our contemporary handshake needs very little space as compared to the formal bow of a seventeenth-century gentleman or the necessary poses of both the ladies and the gentlemen. Moreover, the sense of flair with its corresponding need for space may be viewed as part of the previously discussed sense of overall adornment or artifice. The personal display, the elaborate fashion, the florid speech, and the dancelike, indeed dance-influenced, deportment and physical manners are all a part of the same overall aesthetic of a highly adorned society.

GENERAL PHYSICAL AND MOVEMENT CONCERNS

To begin, it must be understood that re-creating the movement of most any historical period relies somewhat on intelligent guesswork. As noted previously, for the period of the Restoration, we are quite fortunate in that there remain many primary sources that define the various physical mandates of deportment. The handbooks left us by dancing masters and the various guides to deportment delineate the execution of bows, curtsies, walking, sitting, and so on. Additionally, the portraiture and the other artwork of the period provide excellent insight into physical bearing and carriage of the era. However, as helpful as all these sources are, they do not provide a complete picture of all movement and gesture, or at least not enough for the actor to develop an entire physical life for his character. Thus, many of the following descriptions of movement and suggested exercises rely partially on conjecture to fill in when necessary. Further, it should be noted that all explanations are conveyed with modern theatrical production in mind, and, thus, may at times be more theatrical than historically accurate.

In this era of peacock excess in fashion and language, there are a great many adjectives that can be ascribed to a description of the overall bearing or deportment of the body for the ladies and gallants. When the body is at rest (sitting or standing) there is a sense of elegance, self-assurance, poise, lightness, and ease. Conversely, there is clearly a sense of posing, and to our contemporary eyes, flair. When dynamic, the body can be described as elegant, self-assured, graceful, poised, and light, also possessing a sense of flair, display, and, of course, ease. Further, when moving, there is always an awareness of self-presentation. When the physical lives of these Restoration characters are performed well, it seems that the characters are engaged in a dance of sorts. The elegant turn of the wrist, the gracefully turned-out leg, the upright stance, the calculated asymmetry of posture, the tossing of curls, the deep, seductive curtsy, the gracious bow, the clever fan work, and the self-conscious ritual of snuff taking create an elegant choreography for the characters to engage in a graceful dance of life. Perhaps Lyn Oxenford summarizes it best when she claims, "The Restoration play demands a flourish like a dashing signature written in scarlet ink with an ultra-broad nib."[5]

In performing the comedies, it can be concluded that the previous descriptions apply clearly to the true wits and the false wits, the only differences lying in the degree of display or flair. In fact, a portrayal of the false wits can be viewed in light of taking any of these adjectives and pushing them further. Additionally, the fop maintains a profound sense of self-assurance that his or her elaborated bearing is more correct and more graceful than the other inhabitants of his or her world. Conversely, when considering the movement of the witless, it can be gleaned that these attributes of movement are attempted but not achieved, or are ignored, unknown, or openly defied. Thus, in this chapter, after the Laban-based explorations into the overall styles of movement for the true wits, the false wits, and the witless, all postures, carriages, courtesies, and other forms of nonverbal communication will be delineated for persons of quality (the true wits). Within each discussion, suggestions will be made for possible movement choices for portrayal of the false wits. Suggestions will not be made for choices for the witless, as most of these characters either ignore or choose not to emulate the physical bearing of the polite world. Thus, with respect to the few characters who try but do not achieve the grace of the true wits, the attempt and subsequent failure to succeed in the postures, carriages, and gestures is enough.

A LABAN APPROACH

To commence the physical and movement work for this unit, it is recommended that a warm-up using the basic "Experimenting with Laban" exercises delineated in Chapter 4 be used, particularly the first two parts of these exercises. Upon reviewing the overall descriptions of the dynamic and static body for gentlefolk of this period (graceful, poised, elegant, self-assured, light, easy, and exuding flair), it becomes apparent that working with Laban's light effort actions will be most helpful in attaining this overall sense or style of movement. Therefore, it is suggested that in this warm-up, attention be paid especially to the Glide, the Dab, the Flick, and the Float.

Exercises

Finding the Lightness Through Opposition

1. Find the Press by performing step 1 of the Press exercise. At the point when the body is fully engaged in moving the large, heavy object across the room, allow the object to suddenly become very light, almost weightless. Since the object is very large, it still requires much, if not all, of the body to move it from one side of the

room to the other. Further, imagine ice-skating while coaxing the object across the room. Experiment with as many different parts of the body as possible to continue the motion, noticing the grace with which this action may be achieved. Suddenly, and for a brief period of time, the object once again becomes very heavy. Return to the effort necessary to continue the action. After a brief interval, the object returns to its almost weightless state. Continue the graceful gliding journey, and relish the ease of motion. This sequence may be repeated as desired.

2. Explore the Punch with several parts of the body, as if you are engaged in a workout with a hanging punching bag. Continue until the entire body has become engaged. Then allow the punching bag to transform into a wall-sized, very delicate canvas, on which you are painting with various parts of your body. Not only is the canvas delicate, but the paints are extremely precious and costly. Finally, the entire process of painting is a performance for an admiring audience. Dab the priceless paint onto your canvas with hands, feet, nose, elbow, and so on, with a keen sense of assurance, pride, flair, and ease, all for the benefit of your adoring audience. At some point, the canvas again transforms into the punching bag for a brief period of time, and then back into the canvas for a longer period. Again, this may be repeated as desired.

3. Explore the Slash by imagining you are cutting a path through heavy vegetation, alternately using different individual parts of the body or two or more at once. After exploring many parts of the body, the jungle vegetation transforms to a jungle of tiny, thin, fragile balloons. As the balloons seemingly rain down, traverse the space while flicking away these tiny balloons with hands, fingers, toes, elbows, chin, nose, knees, and so on. Relish the ease with which you can perform this, and begin to notice the elegance others achieve in performing this same action. Admire their elegance, all the while taking note of the admiring glances you are receiving. Continue in the sequence suggested in steps 1 and 2.

4. Experiment with the Wring by imaging that you have drunk a poisonous drink that is gradually contorting and crippling the various joints of your skeletal structure. While traversing the space, the body takes on more and more tension as it becomes progressively deformed. Continue to twist, writhe, and basically, wring through the space. Suddenly, with the inspiration of several long, deep breaths, the body becomes progressively lighter, until it is weightless. The joints unbend and loosen, becoming infinitely pliable.

Relish the ease with which the body now floats directionless about the room. Undertake short actions within the room, such as stroking a wall, shaking someone's hand, or walking with a friend. Notice the poise and elegance with which these tasks may be executed. Continue experimenting as delineated in steps 1 and 2.

Experimenting with Laban for Movement of the True Wits

1. Commence moving about the room in a simple and relaxed, easy stride. The tempo should be moderate. Choosing either the Glide or the Float as the primary effort action governing your style of movement, continue to walk around the room. The walk may be considered an easy, strolling stride with a keen sense of lightness instilled by the Glide or the Float. At all times, allow the arms to stay at or above waist level. As the stroll continues, choose to allow flicking or dabbing to enter the overall movement, particularly through the hands, arms, and chin. Women may also try the Flick or the Dab with their toes. These effort actions must remain secondary, while the overall, guiding one is that of the Float or the Glide. Let the small Flicks or the Dabs of the arms, hands, chin, and toes become the means by which interaction with others occurs. Experiment with allowing the Float to remain primary for a time and then switch to the Glide.

2. Next, for integrating vocal and text work with the physical, memorize one of the following short passages from the plays. Continue with step 1 while speaking the text as you move, repeating it as long as the exercise continues. As you glide or float the body and voice, choose specific words to punctuate with the Flick or the Dab. You may stop briefly in the movement to communicate (in part or wholly) your text to another.

HORNER, FROM WYCHERLEY'S COUNTRY WIFE

A mistress should be like a little country retreat near the town; not to dwell in constantly, but only for a night and away, to taste the town the better when the man returns.

MEDLEY, FROM ETHEREGE'S MAN OF MODE

Bawds are as much out of fashion as gentlemen-ushers; none but old formal ladies use the one, and none but foppish old stagers employ the other. Go! You are an insignificant brandy bottle.

ARCHER, FROM FARQUHAR'S BEAUX' STRATAGEM

Madam, the ladies pay best; the honour of serving them is sufficient wages; there is a charm in their looks that delivers a pleasure with their commands, and gives our duty the wings of inclination.

AMANDA, FROM VANBRUGH'S *RELAPSE*

I could never yet perceive the town inclined to part with any of its diversions for the sake of there being crimes; but I have seen it very fond of some I think had little else to recommend them.

MRS. MARWOOD, FROM CONGREVE'S *WAY OF THE WORLD*

Shame and ingratitude! Do you reproach me? You, you upbraid me! Have I been false to her, through strict fidelity to you, and sacrificed my friendship to keep my love inviolate?

MRS. SULLEN, FROM FARQUHAR'S *BEAUX' STRATAGEM*

O Sister, Sister! If ever you marry, beware of a sullen, silent sot, one that's always musing, but never thinks. There's some diversion in a talking blockhead; and since a woman must wear chains, I would have the pleasure of hearing 'em rattle a little.

Experimenting with Laban for Movement of the False Wits

1. Commence moving about the room in a simple, relaxed, easy stride. The tempo should be moderate. Choosing either the Float or the Glide as the primary effort action governing your style of movement, continue to walk around the room. As you move about, keeping your arms at or above waist level, allow the Flick and the Dab to enter into your overall movement style, both in your walk and into your arms. As you attempt to maintain the ease and grace of the Float or the Glide, the Flick and/or the Dab keep insinuating themselves and gradually become more prominent. As the exercise continues, the carriage may vacillate between the more graceful effort actions to the more percussive ones; however, the Flick and the Dab should become primary. Overall, the walk may be considered a prance, but at all times remains the walk of a human being.

   An alternative is to float or glide gracefully around the room, relishing the exquisite beauty of your movement. Flaunt your grace, all the while acknowledging that you are the most graceful person in the room. As you interact physically with others, display your keen agility and ease.

   Another alternative is to move about the room informed predominantly by the Flick or the Dab, savoring the great delicacy of your carriage and deportment. Display to others the lightness, grace, and ease of these percussive gestures.

2. Next, choose one of the following passages to integrate as the movement continues. Experiment with the vacillation between the graceful effort actions of the Float and the Glide and the more percussive ones of the Flick and the Dab, allowing these two

to predominate. Allow certain words or sounds to be punctuated vocally and physically, by displaying your facility in flicking and dabbing.

MR. SPARKISH, FROM WYCHERLEY'S COUNTRY WIFE

I love to be envied, and would not marry a wife that I alone could love; loving alone is as dull as eating alone. Is it not a frank age? And I am a frank person; and to tell you the truth, it may be I love to have rivals in a wife...

SIR FOPLING FLUTTER, FROM ETHEREGE'S MAN OF MODE

All the world will be in the Park to-night. Ladies, 'twere pity to keep so much Beauty longer within doors and rob the Ring of all those charms that should Adorn it.

LADY FIDGET, FROM THE COUNTRY WIFE

... you men report such things of yourselves, one does not know how or whom to believe; and it is come to that pass we dare not take your words no more than your tailor's, without some staid servant of yours be bound with you.

LADY WISHFORT, FROM CONGREVE'S WAY OF THE WORLD

Frippery? Superannuated frippery! I'll frippery the villain; I'll reduce him to frippery and rags. A tatterdemalion! I hope to see him hung with tatters, like a long Lane penthouse, or a gibbet-thief.

Experimenting with Laban for the Movement of the Witless

1. Commence moving about the room in an easy, relaxed stride. As you move about, imagine the atmosphere becoming very thick and heavy. As it becomes increasingly difficult to move through space, allow the Press or the Wring to become your primary effort action defining your movement through space. Further, attempt to conquer the heavy atmosphere by attempting to float or glide, yet the density overtakes you, forcing you back into a pressing or wringing carriage and gait. Try to keep the arms up above the waist, using them to communicate with others through the Dab and the Flick. Here too, the density of the air weighs on you, usually requiring you to rely on the Slash and the Punch. Attempt to emulate what you believe the others to be demanding of you: to float, glide, flick, and dab. However, as you attempt these actions, they usually are manifested in their opposite heavy effort actions. After trying for a time to accomplish the accepted modes of movement, give up on the effort and relish your own style of pressing, wringing, slashing, and punching.
2. Memorize one of the following short passages. As you move about the room, speaking and utilizing primarily the Wring and the Press

to define your overall movement, choose words to emphasize with the Punch and the Slash. After a short while, attempt to utilize the light effort actions to define and emphasize your voice and movement, but the process is an extremely difficult one, as your body and voice are very heavy and lack agility. As you attempt the light effort actions, play against the obstacle of the heavier effort actions. Attempt to impress the other participants with your grace and ease, but the attempt is strenuous as the heavy actions continue to break into your display.

SIR SIMON ADDLEPLOT, FROM WYCHERLEY'S LOVE IN A WOOD

... she is as arrant a Jilt, as ever pull'd pillow from under husbands head (faith and troth) moreover she is bow-legg'd, hopper-hipp'd, and betwixt Pomatum and Spanish Red, has a Complexion like a Holland cheese, and no more Teeth left, than such as give a Haust-goust to her breath; but she is rich (faith and troth).

MISS HOYDEN, FROM VANBRUGH'S RELAPSE

... it's well I have a husband a-coming, or I'cod, I'd marry the baker, I would so. Nobody can knock at the gate, but presently I must be locked up; and here's the young greyhound bitch can run loose about the house all day long, she can; 'tis very well.

MISS PRUE, FROM WYCHERLEY'S PLAIN DEALER

... and I'll speak truth, tho' one should always tell a lie to a man; and I don't care, let my father do what he will; I'm too big to be whipt, so I'll tell you plainly, I don't like you, nor love you at all, nor never will, what's more: So, there's your answer for you; and don't trouble me no more, you ugly thing.

MANLY, FROM THE PLAIN DEALER

... but I, that am an unmannerly Seafellow, if I ever speak well of people (which is very seldom indeed) it shou'd be sure to be behind their backs; and if I wou'd justle a proud, strutting, over-looking Coxcomb, at the head of his Sycophants, rather than put out my tongue at him, when he were past me; wou'd frown in the arrogant, big, dull face of an overgrown Knave of business, rather than vent my spleen against him, when his back were turn'd.

SIR JOHN BRUTE, FROM VANBRUGH'S PROVOK'D WIFE

Oons, Sir, I think a Woman and a Secret, are the two Impertinentest Themes in the Universe. Therefore pray let's hear no more, of my Wife nor your Mistress. Damn 'em both with all my Heart, and every thing else that Daggle a Petticoat, except four Generous whores, with Betty Sands at the head of 'em who were drunk with my Lord Rake and I, ten times in a Fortnight.

POSTURES DELINEATED

The Gentleman

Overall, the ideal bearing of the male body at rest was one of calculated ease and elegance. It was incumbent upon the gentlemen to employ artful and elegant placements and postures of the body in order to appear to be at ease at all times. One of the greatest compliments of the day was to be considered easy in bearing and deportment. The graceful turnout of the leg placed "just so" while standing should not convey a sense of overt self-consciousness. The bend of the elbow and arch of the wrist to display a particularly beautiful, lace-trimmed handkerchief should communicate, "My arm has simply relaxed into this position." One of the prominent dancing masters who propagated this sense of artful elegance, Kellom Tomlinson, noted:

> Let us imagine ourselves, as so many living pictures drawn by the most excellent masters, exquisitely designed to afford the utmost pleasure to beholders; and indeed, we ought to set our bodies in such a disposition when we stand in conversation, that, were our actions or postures delineated, they might bear the strictest examination of the most critical judges."[6]

However, it was a fine line that was drawn between the successful achievement of the necessary physical grace and slavish imitation of the rules for posture, carriage, and overall deportment. The true gentleman conveyed a sense that his manners (much like his clothing) fell on him gently, even loosely, and without affectation, whereas the person who became a slave to all the particulars of deportment and manners imported from France, and who strutted and flaunted his dexterity and skill in the execution of such, was an object of scorn.

Standing, Sitting, and Walking

First, and of primary importance, is the need to stand with an erect, lengthened spine and a *sternum lead*, or that which we consider good or proper posture for effective speaking and acting. Not only was slouching or collapsing the spine not considered genteel in this period, the clothing, with the long waistcoat and heavier outer coat, needed to be supported in order to be displayed in its best possible line. At the top of the spine, the neck should also feel lengthened (particularly in the back) with the head held high on the first vertebra. It should be noted that a sternum lead or an elevated sternum does not imply an overly arched lower back, a particular habit adopted when one is initially required to bear the weight of the clothing. When working on this posture, it is helpful to remember to engage the abdominal muscles slightly to prevent this arching, so as to protect the lower back from strain.

When standing in casual conversation, it was acceptable for the arms to hang loosely in a relaxed manner at the sides. However, there are variations on this posture that seem to have been deemed more aesthetically pleasing by the dancing masters and arbiters of etiquette. The arms may also fall casually onto the hips. A favored version was for one arm to be on the hip, with the other arm bent at the elbow and opened out slightly away from the body. The wrist was gently curved, often with a lovely handkerchief dangling from the fingers extending from an upturned palm. The bent arm that curves gracefully onto the hip might hold one's hat, especially later in the period when, because of the popularity of wigs, the hat was not always kept on one's head. The bent position of the arms is also useful in revealing the heavy, elegant sleeves of one's coat, the fine, elaborate lace at one's wrist, as well as a particularly beautiful pair of gloves. The free hand also becomes an effective tool for gesture. One hand may also relax at the top of the sword hilt or be tucked delicately into the opening of the waistcoat just below the chest area so that the bent arm forms nearly a ninety-degree angle.

For the false wit, the overall look can be greatly enhanced by an abundance of lace at the wrist cuff or a remarkably gaudy handkerchief to dangle from the upturned fingers. Further, the fop may choose to gesticulate more freely and more floridly with his free hand than a true wit would ever consider, taking more pains to display his finery not-so-nonchalantly.

With respect to the legs, the main component that runs through all the etiquette handbooks and books of the dance masters is the need for the feet to be "well turned." Upon closer scrutiny of portraiture and paintings, and considering the close association of genteel deportment with dance, it becomes quite clear that this turning of the feet is that which is considered *turnout* in classical ballet. That is, the femur is rotated in the hip joint and the entire leg (including the foot) is turned out. Although it was allowable for the legs to be symmetrical and held directly under the hips (in what may be considered a somewhat narrow second position), a more asymmetrical pose was clearly favored, with one leg placed directly under the torso and one leg stepped slightly forward. With both legs turned out, the position approximates the fourth position of ballet. The weight in this position is on the back leg, which presents a wonderful opportunity to "make a leg" with the forward leg. That is, the gentleman is free to display his well-turned calf by tensing the muscles of the calf in the forward leg. It was also acceptable to shift the weight equally onto both legs in this position. Finally, the picture was completed by displaying an elegant pair of red-heeled shoes. See Figure 5–6 for a frontal view of a gentleman standing.

FIGURE 5–6 Gentleman Standing © 2001 by Arthur Dirks

When standing and conversing, an attractive asymmetrical line can be achieved not only by employing the approximated fourth position but also by a non-full-frontal presentation. That is, the sides of the hip and leg may be focused toward the other person. At the same time, the upper chest area, neck, head, and extended hand will also turn somewhat to the other person. Onstage, this presentation helps create an interesting asymmetrical picture.

For the false wit, standing offers bountiful opportunity to flaunt one's "regal" bearing. He may, for instance, display an extreme amount of turnout or draw more attention than is warranted to his forward calf by frequently flexing and relaxing the calf muscle. He may also change poses more often than the true wits.

When sitting, the erect stature of the torso is maintained, as is the desired asymmetry. Before lowering into a chair, the rear of one's coat must be flipped out to the sides so that the coat is not sat upon. Further, the sword must be manipulated quickly and gently to the side of the chair. It is ideal when these two actions can be executed as economically as possible so that they meld into one action. As the hands move to the tails or sides of one's coat, the sword is pushed or gently touched into position. So that the fabric of the breeches might not be strained, it was also important to sit on the edge of a chair, even if one's upper back were to lounge slightly into the back of a chair. Sitting provided an excellent opportunity to display a well-turned calf. One leg could be slid under or just into the front of a chair, and the other slid forward while maintaining the turnout. Figure 5–7 delineates the primary seated posture for a gentleman.

It was also acceptable for one leg to be brought up and delicately placed on the knee of the other. (See Figure 5–8.) This is not the same posture as modern times, in which the knees are crossed; the supporting knee would hit at about mid-calf area of the raised and turned-out leg. However, this posture would not be used when women were present. The arms in all of these postures assumed the same positions of the standing body. Finally, the art of sitting, as well as rising, had to be carefully honed into actions of effortless grace, since the gentleman was required to rise whenever any other person of quality in his presence did so.

Here too, the false wit finds ample opportunity to flaunt his graceful posture. All the details of arranging oneself into the chair (the working of the coat and the sword, the lowering, and the arrangement of the legs and arms) may all be accomplished with much more flair—with much more superfluous gesture—than is required. Little flourishes of the hands may be inserted in between movements to destroy any sense of economy.

FIGURE 5–7 Gentleman Seated © 2001 by Arthur Dirks

Walking was merely an extension or animation of the standing posture delineated earlier. With both legs in turnout, there was a sense of
presenting the leg, all the while displaying the inside of the calf. This
presentation of the leg, combined with the wearing of swords and long
coats of somewhat heavy, luxurious fabrics, contributed to what many
writers have referred to as a *swinging gait*. However, although there was
clearly a need to deal with the swinging of a sword and the manipulation

FIGURE 5–8 Gentleman Seated (alternate position)
© 2001 by Arthur Dirks

of the legs through the fabric and cut of the coat, the desire to present an aesthetically pleasing dynamic body seemed to outweigh the practical concerns.

When considering and practicing the walk, it is best to first look at the actual gait and then to add the position of the arms. Standing in the very erect, asymmetrical posture with the weight on the back leg and both legs well turned out, the weight shifts forward onto the front leg and foot, while the rear leg rises up and forward. First, the heel is removed and then the toes. Stepping onto the leading foot is executed by receiving the weight first onto the heel and then rolling onto the toes. This may not seem much different from what we consider to be ordinary walking today; however, there are four things to be considered: the turnout of the legs and feet, the conscious presentation of the calf, the working through from heel to toe, and the soft pointing of the toes as they disengage from the floor. All of this amounts to a forward presentation of the leg, leading with the heel, stepping onto the heel, and rolling onto the toe as the heel lifts off the ground. (Figure 5–9 shows a gentleman in mid-stride.) It should feel as if the inside of the calves are pushing forward. The knees should not lock, but remain somewhat loose or soft. However, after the rear leg is lifted and moves forward, it is straightened (but not hyperextended) before the heel engages with the floor. The comical deep bend and pronounced heel lead often associated with the movement in the commedia dell'arte should be avoided. Further, there should be no sense of bobbing or bouncing. In a friendly stroll about town or the mall, men were advised to maintain a civil pace and not stride too widely. They were also instructed to give the wall side of a roadway to a person of higher rank or to a lady. If there were no walls or if strolling indoors, such as in a gallery of a large home, the superior was to be kept to one's right side at all times. Gentlemen were also admonished never to yell to a friend when in the presence of a person of rank, but to offer only a subtle salutation (bow). Finally, when walking with a woman, it was acceptable for the gentleman to lead the lady by the hand.

With respect to the arms while walking, an elegant ease was to be maintained. It was acceptable to allow the arms to fall into a very gentle and subtle natural swing at one's sides. However, this motion allowed the lace at one's wrist to fall over the hands and sometimes for the heavy coat sleeves to swing unattractively. Thus, another favored version was to allow one hand to rest on the hip or the sword hilt, while the other arm maintained the upturned, open position for standing.

For the fop, walking can be an occasion, indeed, a parade. He may, in fact, prance rather than stride, with the forward movement more influenced by flicking than gliding or floating. The leg may be extended sooner than is necessary, so that the display of the inner calf is more

FIGURE 5–9 Gentleman in Stride © 2001 by Arthur Dirks

pronounced, and the toes may point severely as they disengage from the ground. Arms may move in ongoing flourishes of flowery gesture.

However, for both true wit and false wit, it is important to understand that in these upright, dancelike postures for standing, sitting, and walking, the body should not feel restricted or tensed. With the slight sternum lift and the slightly engaged abdominal muscles, the head should swivel easily from one side to the other. The shoulders should remain relaxed and not hunch up. When standing or sitting, the torso should be capable of swiveling easily to one side or the other. Additionally, when standing in the asymmetrical position, if the body is free enough, one should be capable of shifting the weight from the ball of one foot to the other and readily pivoting the entire body's focus from one side to the other (from facing front to facing back).

The Gentlewoman

For the ladies, an overall sense of grace and ease was equally as important as it was for the gentlemen. Truly, with the new fashion of clothing imported from France, women attained far more ease in movement than in the previous century. In particular, the head, neck, shoulders, and arms could be held with less tension and had a much wider range of motion. However, this freedom did not extend to the ribcage, as noted earlier, and women dealt with even more confinement of the torso than did the men. Overall, women also sought to portray a sense of ease and naturalness in their bearing (despite the restriction imposed by undercloth-ing), all the while aware of the artful picture they were presenting. Here, too, the sense of calculated casualness and elegance was important. In some ways, this sense of calculation even surpassed that of the men. The myriad of nuances displayed by the subtle gestures of tossing a cluster of curls or lowering one's eyelids, for example, were entirely calculated and well honed. As with the men, the women also had to be very careful they did not flaunt their deportment to the point of excess. John Essex, in his *Dancing Master*, cautioned:

> If she holds her head upright, and the body well disposed, without affectation, or too much boldness, they say, There goes a stately lady. If she carries it negligently, they accuse her of carelessness; if she pokes her head forward, of indolence; and in short if she stoops, of thoughtlessness, or want of assurance; and so on.[7]

Standing, Sitting, and Walking

As for the men, women must also consider the upright, stacked spine as integral to the basic posture. For women, however, the task is a bit simpler to achieve, having the added advantage of corsets. One will readily discover that it is quite difficult, if not painful, to try to let the spine bend, slouch, or collapse in any way, as these more relaxed postures may force a corset bone into one's ribcage. However, it is still necessary to include the neck in this sense of stacking the spine, so that it stays lengthened at the back. The idea of the sternum lead is equally important for women, since if there is any collapsing at the top of the torso onto the corset or boned bodice, the overall visual effect is one of inelegance. Further, the shoulders must remain relaxed and slightly back, with the arms held a few inches away from the body. Additionally, this posture drew attention to that area of the body which was most displayed by the fashion of the era, the décolletage. Like the men, although arms could at times fall elegantly to one's sides, such as in the execution of a curtsy, this was not a favored position overall. The width of the skirts, the adornment of sleeves, and the necessary personal props of fan and mask often necessitated other placements. From portraiture and other paintings, it seems that a customary pose was to hold the closed fan, or the fan and the mask, in front of the body at the bottom edge of the stiffened bodice. The fan would be held in one hand (seemingly the right) and placed into the upturned palm of the other hand. (The positions of the fan will be covered in a subsequent section within this chapter.) Elbows are gracefully bent and held just away from the body. Another variation is for one hand to be held at the lower edge of the bodice while the other hangs loosely off to the side, slightly away from the body so as not to crush sleeves and the skirt.

With respect to the legs and feet, again, turnout is necessary. The feet may be together and turned out (with heels together and toes apart), as in the first position of ballet; or, a small step may be taken slightly forward onto one foot so that the feet are only slightly apart, the distance not being as large as for the men's standing posture. This may be considered a modified third position of ballet. Figure 5–10 demonstrates the standing posture in first position, with the hands holding a fan at the lower edge of the bodice. Note the very upright posture, the turnout, and the graceful arms.

The idea of asymmetrical presentation also comes into play when a lady is standing and conversing. Although the full-frontal presentation was considered quite appropriate, the asymmetry is documented in the many portraits and other paintings of the period. While the woman's body is in the proper standing stance, an elegant turn of the neck and head accompanied by a gentle turn of the shoulders and chest is executed to one side or the other.

For the female false wit, again visual presentation will aid immensely. Costuming that includes more lace, more color, more texture, or basically, more anything, will not only set these characters apart from the

FIGURE 5–10 Lady Standing © 2001 by Arthur Dirks

true wits, but will allow the actor more opportunity for her sense of display. When standing, the female false wit may, perhaps, never demonstrate a sense of calm or complete ease, but rather one of restrained agitation, as is particularly appropriate for the likes of Lady Fidget in *The Country Wife*. Another defining choice might be to have the false wit rely solely on full-frontal presentation, while the true wits gracefully work off to the sides of their torsos.

Sitting was not so difficult a task as it was in the previous century, with skirts formed and stiffened by farthingales. However, in spite of the softer, less-structured skirts of the Restoration, the stiffened bodices, the sheer amount of fabric worn, and particularly the guides to deportment necessitated that a lady sit on the edge of a chair in an erect position. If a train were being worn, the lady must approach the chair in a small, semicircular pattern and make a small turn or pivot in order not to become twisted into her train, movements requiring much practice so that the chair was not missed altogether. Here, too, hands and arms could fall elegantly to one's sides, slightly away from the body, but the most commonly accepted position was one in which the woman held her fan in one hand and placed it into the opened palm of the other, both hands held at the lower edge of the bodice. The fan could be held in a variety of positions, which will be delineated later in this chapter. With respect to the shoulders, neck, and head, the same poise and ease of the standing posture were to be maintained. Finally, the *peeping toe* was in vogue throughout the Restoration era and into the eighteenth century. While the lady was seated, the toe of one slipper was elegantly slid forward so that about half the foot was exposed from under the skirts. Figure 5–11 shows a side view of a lady sitting.

When it came to walking, women were cautioned to take small, elegant steps, maintaining an easy, graceful stride. From early on, the dance master taught his pupils the rudiments of correct walking. Many hours were spent with the dance master holding a girl's hands as he guided her to walk toward him in tiny steps, with the feet well turned out. She was to attempt to walk in a straight line, keeping one foot close to the other. It was imperative that a woman also maintain all the stature associated with simple standing. Athene Seyler captures the essence of seventeenth-century ladies' carriage and gait in her *Craft of Comedy*, noting, "I should say that woman ought to *dance* as she moves in a seventeenth-century play."[8] Figure 5–12 depicts a lady in stride, highlighting the turnout and the necessary small steps.

There were a few added considerations when a gentlewoman walked. First, the length of the skirt often made it necessary for the walker to initiate little kicks against the front of the skirt's bottom, so that she would not stumble. If walking outside, particularly in inclement weather, the

FIGURE 5–11 Lady Sitting © 2001 by Arthur Dirks

FIGURE 5–12 Lady in Stride © 2001 by Arthur Dirks

outer skirt might be tucked up into the underskirt to protect the fabric, forcing the lady to manage the extra layers of bundled fabric. Even though the longer, more formal trains were out of vogue for most of the Restoration (except when attending ceremonies at court), shorter, more informal trains were still often attached to skirts. Outdoors, this necessitated that the trains be either pulled up with stays or ribbons from the shoulders or carried by a page who walked behind the lady, yet another consideration particularly with respect to the tempo of one's gait. Even shorter trains might be worn indoors, but they still necessitated handling. The navigation through space became particularly important, requiring circular movements in order not to step on one's gown. Further, the lady must master the technique of carefully and elegantly picking up her skirt in order to step up or down, or in order to navigate corners and tight spaces. Additionally, the skirt was not merely lifted, but all touching and placement of the fabric was performed with a sense of display as the skirt moved with an elegant sweep. All of the gestures used to manipulate one's clothing functioned as an opportunity to display a sumptuous wardrobe.

The false wit, sitting and walking, can be a study in more *percussive*, rather than *legato*, movement. She may not float or glide into a chair or across the mall; rather, she may dab little steps and flick her skirts forward. She may also take more time than a true wit would with the self-conscious flaunting of her elegant clothing.

Like the men, the women also must maintain this erect posture and carriage without undue tension. Again, by engaging the abdominal muscles, much tension may be removed from the back. Further, the neck, head, and shoulders must also remain loose and free to move. With the arms held away from the body to keep them free of the torso, it is also necessary to ensure that the shoulders are not hunching up with undue tension in the trapezius muscles. Finally, an important word concerning corsets must be inserted when considering unnecessary tension: With the wearing of these period corsets (or an approximation of such), it is imperative that the actor can maintain a sense of lower rib expansion or *rib swing* when breathing. No corset should be constructed or laced so tightly as to inhibit the necessary expansion for breathing and speaking.

Exercises: Discovering the Posture and Carriage

The Standing Posture

Standing erect, with your spinal column stacked one vertebra atop another and with feet equidistant from center under your hips, on the inspiration of a breath, allow the sternum to float slightly toward the ceiling.

As you inhale, allow the shoulders to follow the sternum, but then on the exhalation, let them fall very slightly back and down. Make sure there is a slight engagement of the abdominal wall, but not a strong "sucked in" sensation. On another breath, slightly rise up on the balls of the feet; and then on the exhalation, allowing the entire leg to turn out in the hip socket, let the heels angle in toward each other and lower to the floor, so that you are in the first position of ballet.

FOR THE MEN

The next step is for men only. On another inhalation, rise up onto the balls of the feet and take a small step forward with the right foot, maintaining the turnout at all times. On the exhalation, allow the body to float down (lower the heels) to arrive at the modified fourth position outlined previously.

FOR BOTH MEN AND WOMEN

Next, for both men and women, on an inhalation, let the arms, led by the elbows, float out and away from the sides at about a forty-five-degree angle to the shoulder. The wrist, with hands and fingers gracefully extended, gently follow behind the elbows so that the arms are in a slightly rounded position. On the exhalation, the movement is reversed as the elbows, wrists, and hands gently float back to the sides. Repeat, and after several times, stop halfway, with the arms rounded and out.

FOR MEN

As you exhale, allow the left arm to fall to your left hip and come to rest on the back of the hand, the inside facing back. On the next inhalation, allow the right arm, with a softly bent elbow, to circle in toward your body; as the fingers reach the top of the circle, pointing toward the ceiling, exhale and let the arm—led by the wrist and hand—glide to the open-palmed position with palm facing up and fingers gracefully curved and extended (see Figure 5–6).

FOR WOMEN

As you exhale, allow the hands and arms, maintaining a graceful curve of the elbow, to glide toward the center of the bottom of your bodice. The left hand will glide under the right with an upturned palm, and the right (holding a fan) will glide into the open palm, with the fan extending away and to the left of the body and slightly down (see Figure 5–10).

FOR BOTH MEN AND WOMEN

At this point, it is helpful to take several inhalations and allow the body to float upward on the balls of the feet and the sternum to lift ever so slightly. Then on the exhalations, glide the body down onto the full foot, allowing the shoulders to fall slightly back and down. Relish the ease of this movement.

Walking

FOR MEN

From the previous position, while maintaining the feeling that the entire torso will stay exactly in the middle of both legs, allow the heel of the back leg to glide up with a sense of leading with the calf; the toes disengage, pointing toward the floor, following the heel. With a softly bent knee, the leg continues to glide forward and then straighten before the heel is placed on the floor, allowing the toes also then to float down. As the walking motion continues, it is important to maintain the floating of the sternum slightly upward and for the legs to continually glide through the slightly modified fourth position. However, it is important that the feet lead the movement, not the sternum, so that the leg is always being presented (see Figure 5–9). There should also be a sense that the head is gliding forward at a constant level. At first, the tempo will necessarily seem quite slow, but as the motion becomes easier, be sure to allow the tempo to quicken to an easy, flowing stride.

While experimenting with the walk, it is helpful to stop now and then and float into the standing posture. Further, once stopped in standing position, inhale and allow the body to float up slightly onto the balls of the feet and then pivot to the opposite direction, lowering onto the heels as the breath is exhaled. Once mastered, the stop will occur for a very brief moment as it flows directly into the pivot and then back to walking. Also experiment with reversing arm positions during the pivot, gliding the right hand to the hip and the left in the semicircular float up to the open-palmed position.

When portraying the false wit and experimenting with this exercise, try the following variations:

1. When the leg is gliding forward, bend the knee more than necessary, and then flex the foot quite severely before placing the heel on the floor.
2. Play with fluctuations in tempo.
3. When inhaling for the commencement of any movement, take a deeper breath than necessary, and perform the movement with added flourishes, particularly inspired by the Flick and the Dab. For example, when reversing arm positions, perform a little circular flourish with the wrist prior to placing it in the open-palmed position.
4. Slightly vocalize your exhalations.

FOR WOMEN

From the previous position (outlined on page 137), one heel will float up, followed by the toes, and glide forward in the typical mechanics of walking, with the knees softly bent. However, the entire body must glide forward, the level of the head staying constant at all times. Further, be sure to allow the hips to glide forward as a solid unit or block, sensing the entire trunk moving forward, not the separate parts. This will inhibit any bobbing or swaying. Here, too, the movement is initiated by the legs, and the steps must be kept small (see Figure 5–12). Although the sternum is floated up, do not allow it to lead the walk. Another method of preventing bobbing is to raise and lower the entire foot as a unit, rather than working through the foot from heel to toe—a movement not as necessary for the women as for the men. Additionally, if the length of the skirt requires, a small flicking motion by the toes may be incorporated to keep the front hem of the skirt away from the step. Again, at first the tempo will seem quite slow; but allow it to gradually accelerate as the ease of the movement is achieved. However, a word of caution: the tempo will always be perceived as quite a bit slower than contemporary strolling.

After a time, experiment with walking and then come to the correct standing position, allowing the back leg to glide into first position next to the front leg; or allow the back leg (still turned out) to glide just slightly forward of the front leg. In this alternate position, practice inhaling and floating up onto the balls of the feet and elegantly pivoting to the opposite side. Then exhale and float down into the weight of the entire foot. The walk may then be resumed.

For experimenting with the female false wit, try the following.

1. Raise the sternum slightly more than is necessary in order to display more of the décolletage.
2. Keep the stride based on very small flicked or dabbed steps and allow the body to bounce ever-so-slightly.
3. Experiment with tempo changes, often relying on quick ones.
4. Softly vocalize your exhalations.

Sitting

FOR MEN

While practicing walking, approach a chair or bench and when the front leg is quite close to the front of the furniture, pivot on an inhalation. When the pivot is complete, the back of the rear leg should be touching or very nearly touching the edge of the seat. On the inhalation and all in one movement, let the arms float down, gently sweeping away the fabric of the coat and the sword if one is worn. On the exhalation and as the arms are seemingly suspended out in the air, let the body gently lower to the edge of the chair, maintaining the upright posture and sternum lift. If necessary, on another inhalation, allow the arms to float in a circular motion and then glide on the exhalation to the proper position with one arm on the hip and one in the open-palmed position. On the exhalation, one leg may also be slid forward and one a little further back, so that the forward leg is displaying the open calf (see Figure 5–7). With practice, all motions from the lowering of the body onward can be accomplished on one exhalation.

Try the following as an alternative to the just-described seated posture. Once the body is floated onto the chair's edge and arms are in position, on an inhalation, allow the forward leg to float up and toward the opposite knee, and upon exhaling, glide the outside of the calf onto the knee of the supporting leg. When concluded, the inside of the calf should be facing the ceiling. As usual, it is important to maintain turnout during the execution of this movement (see Figure 5–8).

To rise from the seated position, it is first necessary to slide the forward foot closer into the foot nearest the seat. In the alternate position, lower the leg over the supporting leg to the floor, placing the foot just in front of the foot on the floor. These movements, as well as a slight inclination of the entire torso in order to bring the weight of the trunk over the legs, may be executed on the inhalation. Then on the exhalation, as a unit, the entire torso lifts very gracefully upward. It is important that the lean forward defines only a slight angle away from the seated ninety-degree angle and that the upward float of the torso is not restricted by slouching or bending from the waist. The legs are driving the weight of the trunk upward; the trunk is not propelling or pulling itself up. Since the Restoration gentleman was required to rise whenever anyone else in his presence did so, it is necessary to practice sitting and rising until a sense of ease is attained.

To focus on the false wits, experiment with the following.

1. When pivoting, do so with much flourish and on a large intake of air.
2. Separate each movement with an inhalation and an exhalation.
3. Flick or dab away your coat and your sword.
4. Glide to the seat very slowly to draw attention to yourself.
5. As the arms float to position, circle them twice before arriving at the final position.

FOR WOMEN

While practicing the walk approaching a seat, and after the front leg has landed very close to the front edge of a chair, execute a pivot on an inhalation. Let the arms float gracefully down the sides, sweeping aside the train if one is worn. On the exhalation, the entire body glides downward to the edge of the seat, keeping the entire torso erect at all times. On another inhalation, the arms float in a semicircle upward and glide downward on the exhalation to the standard fan position, the right hand falling into the upturned palm of the left. Also on the exhalation and leading with the toes, one foot may glide every so slightly forward so as to "peek out" from under the front of the skirt (see Figure 5–11). If a long train is being worn, the chair may be approached in the semicircular fashion noted earlier before the pivot is executed, so that the bulk of the fabric will be more to one's side.

To rise, only a slight forward torso lean is required to move the weight of the trunk over the legs. It is important that the entire torso incline forward, keeping the back straight. At the same time and on the inhalation, the forward foot glides in closer to the rear foot. On the exhalation, the entire torso lifts as one unit to a standing position. Here, too, one must be careful of inclining more than is necessary and of bending from the waist. Again, it is the legs that drive the trunk upward.

If working on the movement of the false wit, entertain the following ideas.

1. Execute the pivot very quickly.
2. Flick or dab the fabric of your train or dress aside.
3. Flick the peeping toe forward.
4. Rise very quickly.

INTEGRATING MOVEMENT WITH TEXT AND VOICE

Now that the overall movement style of the period has been explored through the use of Laban's effort actions, and the larger movement concerns associated with standing, walking, and sitting have also been discussed and worked, it is appropriate at this time to review these aspects of movement through an integration of text with movement. It is beneficial for the actor to experience the ways in which the highly defined movement vocabulary supports or interacts with the artificial language of the texts. While performing the following exercises, it is helpful to pay particular attention to how the syntax, the devices of wit, and any particularly artificial passage may be supported or punctuated with movement. Further, after working on several short scenes, it usually becomes apparent that the text, voice, and movement are all one. That is, the artifice in the language, the decorative movement style, and the vocal choices (the variables of speech and the playing of the sounds) all support an overall aesthetic, which incorporates a sense of display (even flamboyance), elegance, and ease.

Exercises

1. Choose and memorize any passage from "Experimenting with Laban for Movement of the True Wits" and "Experimenting with Laban for Movement of the False Wits" in this chapter or any from the previous chapters. Before starting, take note of the various devices of wit and the structure of the language. Keeping the rehearsal room largely open, place a few chairs, benches, and/or settees about the room, leaving a fair amount of open space between the various pieces. Float and glide about the room as a group, using your text to communicate with others. If you are playing a false wit, you may rely predominantly on flicking or dabbing, or may insert these actions frequently into your gestures. Be sure to maintain the posture and carriage outlined previously. Also practice stopping and pivoting to converse with someone behind you. Be sure to allow yourself to float your upper torso (or flick it, if playing a false wit) to one side or the other in order to converse with people off to your sides. Approach the seats and practice floating into a seated position, and then converse with someone standing or sitting near you. Practice rising from your seat in order to discover someone else with whom to converse. If you are playing a false wit, practice some of the suggestions noted earlier. Finally, also try to incorporate the effort actions into your voice, as well as to experiment with the variables of speech and with playing the sounds.

2. With a partner, choose and memorize one of the following short scenes. Again, before starting, take a moment with the text to identify the various devices and structures of speech. As with the previous exercise, start with standing and walking about the room and progress to sitting and rising, all the while using the scene to converse with your partner. As this is an improvised exercise, you need not stage the scene beforehand. Rather, as you speak, find phrases, words, or sounds you might wish to punctuate with pivots or stops. At these moments, also attempt to highlight the phrases, words, or sounds by experimenting with the variables of speech or by utilizing the effort actions to effect a change in your voice. Also incorporate sitting and rising from the seated position.

Texts for the True Wits

DORIMANT AND HARRIET, FROM ETHEREGE'S MAN OF MODE

DORIMANT: Think of making a party, madam; love will engage.

HARRIET: You make me start! I did not think to have heard of love from you.

DORIMANT: I never knew what 'twas to have a settled ague yet, but now and then I have irregular fits.

HARRIET: Take heed! Sickness after long health is commonly more violent and dangerous.

DORIMANT: (*Aside*) I have took the infection from her, and feel the disease now spreading in me. (*To her*) Is the name of love as frightful that you dare not state it!

HARRIET: 'Twill do little execution out of your mouth on me, I am sure.

DORIMANT: It has been fatal—

HARRIET: To some easy women, but we are not all born to one destiny. I was informed you used to laugh at love and not make it.

DORIMANT: The time has been but now I must speak—

HARRIET: If it be on that idle subject, I will put on my serious look, turn my head carelessly from you, drop my lip, let my eyelids fall and hang half o'er my eyes—thus—while you buzz a speech of an hour long in my ear, and I answer never a word. Why do you not begin?

DORIMANT: That the company may take notice how passionately I make advances of love, and how disdainfully you receive 'em!

HARRIET: When your love's grown strong enough to make you bear being laughed at, I'll give you leave to trouble me with it. Till then pray forbear, Sir.

MRS. MARWOOD AND MRS. FAINALL, FROM CONGREVE'S *WAY OF THE WORLD*

MRS. MARWOOD: You hate Mankind?

MRS. FAINALL: Heartily, Inveterately.

MRS. MARWOOD: Your Husband?

MRS. FAINALL: Most transcendantly; ay, tho' I say it, meritoriously.

MRS. MARWOOD: Give me your Hand upon it.

MRS. FAINALL: There.

MRS. MARWOOD: I join with you; what I have said, has been to try you.

MRS. FAINALL: Is it possible? Dost thou hate those Vipers Men?

MRS. MARWOOD: I have done hating 'em; and am now come to despise 'em; the next thing I have to do, is eternally to forget 'em.

MRS. FAINALL: There spoke the Spirit of an Amazon, a Penthesilea.

MRS. MARWOOD: And yet I am thinking sometimes, to carry my Aversion further.

MRS. FAINALL: How?

MRS. MARWOOD: Faith by Marrying; if I cou'd but find one that lov'd me very well, and would be throughly sensible of ill usage; I think I shou'd do my self the violence of undergoing the Ceremony.

MRS. FAINALL: You would not make him a Cuckold?

MRS. MARWOOD: No; but I'd make him believe I did, and that's as bad.

RANGER AND VINCENT, FROM WYCHERLEY'S
LOVE IN A WOOD

RANGER: What, not yet a-bed? Your man is laying you to sleep with Usque-baugh or Brandy, is it not so?

VINCENT: What Punk will not be troubled with you to night, therefore I am, is it not so?

RANGER: I have been turn'd out of doors indeed just now, by a woman, Vincent—

VINCENT: Yes, yes, your women are always such women.

RANGER: A Neighbour of yours, and I'm sure the finest you have.

VINCENT: Prythee do not asperse my neighbourhood with your Acquaintance; 'twould bring a scandal upon an Alley.

RANGER: Nay, I do not know her, therefore I come to you.

VINCENT: 'Twas no wonder, she turn'd you out of doors then; and if she had known you, 'twoud have been a wonder she had let you stay.

Texts for the False Wits

WITWOUD AND PETULANT, FROM CONGREVE'S
WAY OF THE WORLD

WITWOUD: Raillery, Raillery, Madam; we have no Animosity—We hit off a little wit now and then, but no Animosity—the falling out of Wits is like the falling out of Lovers—We agree in the main, like Treble and Bass. Ha, Petulant?

PETULANT: Ay, in the main—But when I have a Humour to contradict—

WITWOUD: Ay, when he has a Humour to contradict, then I contradict too. What, I know my cue. Then we contradict one another like two Battle-dores: For Contradictions beget one another like Jews.

PETULANT: If he says Black's Black—if I have a Humour to say 'tis blue—Let that pass—All's one for that. If I have a Humour to prove it, it must be granted.

WITWOUD: Not positively must—But it may—It may.

PETULANT: Yes, it positively must, upon Proof positive.

WITWOUD: Ay, upon Proof positive it must; but upon Proof presumptive it only may. That's a Logical Distinction now, Madam . . .

PETULANT: Importance is one thing, and learning's another; but a debate's a debate, that I assert.

WITWOUD: Petulant's an enemy to learning; he relies altogether on his parts.

PETULANT: No, I'm no enemy to learning; it hurts not me . . . No, no, it's no enemy to anybody but them that have it.

MRS. SQUEAMISH, MRS. DAINTY FIDGET, AND LADY FIDGET, FROM WYCHERLEY'S *COUNTRY WIFE*

MRS. SQUEAMISH: Ay, one would think men of honour should not love, no more than marry, out of their own rank.

MRS. DAINTY FIDGET: Fy, fy, upon 'em! They are come to think cross breeding for themselves best, as well as for their dogs and horses.

LADY FIDGET: They are dogs and horses for't!

MRS. SQUEAMISH: One would think, if not for love, for vanity a little.

MRS. DAINTY FIDGET: Nay, they do satisfy their vanity upon us sometimes; and are kind to us in their report, tell all the world they lie with us.

LADY FIDGET: Damned rascals, that we should be only wronged by 'em! To report a man has had a person, when he has not had a person, is the greatest wrong in the whole world that can be done to a person.

MRS. SQUEAMISH: Well, 'tis an arrant shame noble persons should be so wronged and neglected.

LADY FIDGET: But still 'tis an arranter shame for a noble person to neglect her own honour, and defame her own noble person with little inconsiderable fellows, foh!

MRS. DAINTY FIDGET: I suppose the crime against our honour is the same with a man of quality as with another.

LADY FIDGET: How! No, sure, the man of quality is likest one's husband, and therefore the fault should be the less.

MRS. DAINTY FIDGET: But then the pleasure should be the less.

LADY FIDGET: Fy, fy, fy, for shame, sister! Whither shall we ramble? Be continent in your discourse, or I shall hate you.

MRS. DAINTY FIDGET: Besides, an intrigue is so much the more notorious for the man's quality.

MRS. SQUEAMISH: 'Tis true, nobody takes notice of a private man, and therefore with him 'tis more secret; and the crime's the less when 'tis not known.

LADY FIDGET: You say true; i'faith, I think you are in the right on't: 'tis not an injury to a husband till it be an injury to our honours; so that a woman of honour loses no honour with a private person.

MELANTHA AND PALAMEDE, FROM DRYDEN'S
MARRIAGE A LA MODE

MELANTHA: O, here's her Highness! Now is my time to introduce my self, and to make My court to her, in my new French phrases. Stay, let me read my catalogue—Suitte, figure, chagrin, naivete, and let me die for the Parenthesis of all.

PALAMEDE: (*Aside*) Do, persecute her; and I'll persecute thee as fast in thy own dialect.

MELANTHA: Madam, the Princess! Let me die, but this is a most horrid spectacle to see a person who makes so grand a figure in the Court, without the Suitte of a Princess, and entertaining your Chagrin all alone; (Naivete should have been there, but the disobedient word would not come in.) ...

PALAMEDE: ... (*To Melantha*) let me die, madam, if I have not waited you here these two Long hours, without so much as the Suitte of a single Servant to attend me; entertaining my self with my own Chagrin, till I had the honour to see your Ladiship Who are a person that makes so considerable figure in the Court.

MELANTHA: Truce with your douceurs, good servant; you see I am addressing the Princess; pray do not embarrass me—embarrass me! What a delicious French Word do you make me lose upon you too!

BOWS AND CURTSIES

Because of the records left by dance masters and arbiters of deportment, particularly those of De Lauze and Antoine Courtine, we are fortunate today to be able to reconstruct the mechanics of the execution of the salutations. The extant descriptions not only create quite clear pictures of these movements, but they also substantiate the overall aesthetic of the period. As with walking and sitting, the salutations must be performed with a sense of ease and grace and with a bit of self-consciousness. That is, as reflective of the period's overall sensibility of self-presentation, the bows and curtsies allowed one to demonstrate a sense of calculated casualness or studied negligence. The gentleman's slight sliding forward of the leg and the lady's graceful step to one side drew attention to an elegance that was supposedly innate.

As a means to approach the salutations, the contemporary actor may consider these actions as courtesies of meeting and greeting, and of saying good-bye, similar to modern reliance on the handshake, the embrace, or the friendly kiss. However, since the period was a time of great artifice in presentation and bearing, the gestures differ from contemporary ones in that the handshake of today, for example, does not carry with it a sense of display. Thus, the contemporary actor must embrace the salutations not only as gestures of meeting and greeting, but also as yet another opportunity to flaunt one's genteel bearing.

Finally, it is imperative that the contemporary actor understand when and how *reverences* are to be used. Generally, there are two kinds: the passing bow and curtsy and the more formal bow and curtsy. The first type is employed when meeting another person of quality in passing. It is executed more quickly than the second kind and represents a slight pause in walking. The second and more formal kind is used when entering and leaving a room, upon being introduced to company, when meeting a person of higher rank, and when starting or ending a dance. Reverences are usually instigated by the person of lower rank, or by the man if a man and a woman meet in passing. The formal type also provides the actor with stage business, as these bows and curtsies may also be used to highlight conversation. For example, they may be used to punctuate a win or to concede a loss in a particularly eloquent volley of verbal warfare. When the Millamant and Mirabell scene is analyzed at the end of this chapter, suggestions will be made for various kinds of usage within discourse.

The Passing Bow

The gentleman's passing bow is performed during a brief pause in the walk. While maintaining the turnout of the walk, the leg nearest the person to be saluted slowly moves forward about the length of one step. There may be a slight sensation of sliding. Once the foot has moved forward, there is also a feeling of stopping mid-stride. Assuming the person being approached is on the right, the right leg will step or slide forward. At the same time, the hat is removed with the right hand and placed in the left, where it is held casually at the left hip or under the left arm, with the inside of the hat facing one's body. The right arm may then drop easily down to the right side, while the head is turned to the right toward the approaching company. (If the approaching person is to one's left, the previous instructions are reversed.) Next, the upper body does not bow, but according to the dance masters, there is only a slight bend in both knees while the weight is evenly distributed between both legs. However, a more elegant look may be achieved onstage by bending the back knee more than the front. Further, most actors find this more comfortable mechanically. Figure 5–13 depicts the slight bending of the knees, the graceful drop of the arm, as well as the maintained turnout.

The Formal Bow

As with the bow executed in passing, the hat is removed from the head, always taken by the right and transferred to the left, however. The hat

FIGURE 5–13 Gentleman's Passing Bow © 2001 by Arthur Dirks

is then held at the left hip or under the left arm, as noted earlier. The right foot slides slowly forward, just slightly less than the distance of one step, stopping in the modified fourth position covered in the section on standing. While maintaining the turnout, both knees bend—the back more than the forward one—while the torso, as a unit, inclines forward. That is, the body does not bend at the waist. With the palm facing forward, the right arm sweeps first slightly forward and then elegantly down one's side, without falling behind the line of the body. There is one other aspect of the bow: the kissing of one's own hand that is employed when saluting royalty or women. It may be accomplished in two ways. The right hand may be kissed at the start of the bow before the removal of the hat; or it may be kissed as the bending of the body is commenced. When rising from the bow, as the upper body straightens, the weight of the body moves forward onto the right leg while the left leg takes a small step sideways. The right leg, in turn, steps behind the left to settle in the previously delineated standing position. Figure 5–14a shows the commencement of a bow when the gentleman is preparing to kiss his hand. The right leg has slid forward one step and the torso is just slightly beginning to incline as one unit.

Figure 5–14b reveals the gentleman when he is at the lowest point of the formal bow. The right arm is dropped gracefully; the spine is quite straight; and the rear knee is bent more than the forward knee.

The Passing Curtsy

The lady's passing curtsy also occurs in a brief pause in the course of walking. A small step to the side is taken on the leg farthest from the approaching company, while the body turns slightly toward the approaching person. Again, if the first step is taken to the left, as the weight is removed from the right foot, it pulls into ballet's first position. Next, it slides slightly forward, the distance just less than a small step. A small knee bend, or *demi plié*, is executed while the feet remain well turned out. The torso also inclines slightly forward, while the head stays erect at the top of the spine. As the body rises from the curtsy, the weight moves onto the forward foot; the other foot takes a small step to the side as the body turns to that same side to resume walking. Figure 5–15 demonstrates the slight plié, as well as the erect head.

The Formal Curtsy

This curtsy, though economical in movement, is somewhat more difficult in execution. The lady takes a short step to one side to gain the attention of the person being saluted and then draws the other foot into the heel of the standing foot. Both legs retain turnout, again, resulting in ballet's first

FIGURE 5–14a Gentleman's Formal Bow (begin)
© 2001 by Arthur Dirks

FIGURE 5–14b Gentleman's Formal Bow (complete)
© 2001 by Arthur Dirks

position. A deep bend (or *grand plié*) is then executed, whereby the lady lowers her body. The deepness of the bend is dependent on the occasion and the rank of the other person. If necessary, the heels of the feet may be raised off the floor. At the same time of the bend, the arms glide grace-fully to the sides, falling down toward the floor. The torso then inclines

FIGURE 5–15 Lady's Passing Curtsy © 2001 by Arthur Dirks

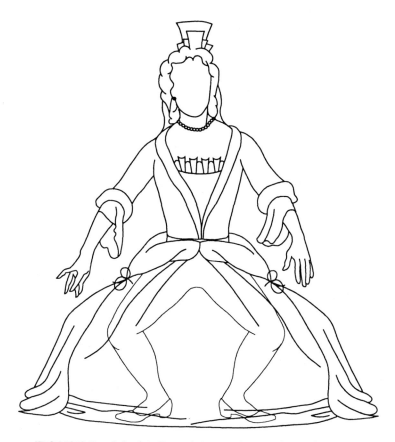

FIGURE 5–16 Lady's Formal Curtsy © 2001 by Arthur Dirks

very slightly forward, while the head remains straight on the spine. To rise, the torso straightens, as do the knees, and the legs drive the body upward. The hands may then return to the position delineated in the section on standing. Figure 5–16 reveals the deep knee bending associated with the formal curtsy, as well as the erect spine and the graceful arms.

Exercises for Experimenting with the Formal Bows and Curtsies

Discovering the Formal Bow

From standing in the typical modified fourth position, take one short step forward onto the left foot as a preparatory step.

1. Inhale while performing the following actions: Circle the right hand inward toward the mouth and mime kissing the hand as it passes by the lips, and then proceed to the rim of the hat. Grasp

the hat and remove it, placing it under the curved left arm, with the lining facing inward. At the same time, glide the right leg slowly forward.

2. On the exhalation, continue with these actions: Let the right arm float down to the right side, being careful not to let it fall behind the line of the body, and bend the torso forward from the pelvis, taking care not to buckle at the waist.

3. Inhale again and proceed as follows: Float the torso back to an upright position, and with the left leg, take one small step diagonally to the side.

4. On the exhalation, perform the following: Float the right arm circularly in toward the body and continue to let it move away from the body to finish in the typical arm position for standing. At the same time, while maintaining turnout, allow the right foot to pull in toward and behind the left foot to arrive at the standing stance. At the completion of this movement, the side of one's body will be slightly angled toward the person who is receiving the bow. Since it was deemed proper for much of the period to converse with the hat on, consider the following alternative: As the right arm circles in toward the body, grasp the corner of the hat and place it back on the head, continuing the circle with the right arm to arrive at the typical stance. However, it should be noted that in stage production, many directors find it more suitable to have the actors hold their hats most of the time so as not to allow stage lighting to cast shadows on their faces.

Discovering the Formal Curtsy

From standing in the typical first position, inhale and perform the following:

1. On the left foot, take one small step to the left and slide the heel of the right foot into the heel of the left foot while maintaining turnout. To avoid bobbing so that the body floats to this new position, it is sometimes helpful to step onto the ball of the left foot and lower the heel as the right foot is gliding in.

2. Allow the arms to begin a natural, graceful fall to the side of the skirt.

Next, exhale while executing the following actions:

1. Maintaining turnout, perform a deep knee bend, or first position *grand plié*, while allowing the air to be slowly and continually expelled. As you lower yourself toward the floor, allow the heels to rise up as necessary. Make sure that the spine is staying completely

erect during the plié, so that the torso is not falling forward or backward.

2. At the same time, allow the arms to continue the graceful downward fall to the sides of the body until they are fully extended downward. It is important that they do not hyperextend; in fact, a very slight curve in the elbows will allow for a small graceful arch of the entire arm. It might be helpful to envision very small inflated balloons between the torso and the inside area of the elbow that keep the arms ever-so-slightly away from the body.

While in the completely lowered position, if the slight torso inclination is desired, it is best to inhale when the torso inclines slightly forward and exhale as it straightens. Before continuing, it is helpful to inhale once more and perform the following on an exhalation:

1. Push through the balls of the feet, propelling the body upward. As soon as possible, lower the heels so that the muscles of the thighs and the hips are now integrated into the upward push until you have arrived at the fully erect position. Again, it is very important that the torso does not incline one way or the other, but that the erect position is maintained throughout.

2. Float the arms, led by the hands, toward the center of the body until they end in the basic fan position delineated earlier.

When experimenting with the bows and curtsies for the false wits, it is important that the basic mechanics of the movements are not seriously altered. The false wits are as adept in these movements as the true wits. Thus, they would not allow the spine to collapse in the course of a bow or a curtsy, nor bring the legs back to an inelegant position for standing, for instance. They might, however, bow or curtsy lower than the occasion demands or stay in the lowered position longer than necessary. Onstage, the lowered position offers the opportunity for the fops to utter lines. They might add little flourishes with the hands when bowing, and the would-be gentleman might also make more of the kissing of his hand during the bow.

GESTURES WITH AND WITHOUT PROPS

In addition to the grosser movements, the physical behavior of the Restoration lady and gentleman was replete with a large repertoire of smaller, subtler gestures, which were used to punctuate a well-turned phrase or to send nonverbal messages. The sniff of a bit of snuff could emphasize the "lesson" portion of an epigram. A touch on the cheek with the fan could suggest an assignation with a potential lover. A fop might toy with his walking stick merely to draw attention to the elaborately carved handle or to signal his boredom; and the flicking aside of a curl would draw attention to a man's new and elaborate full-bottomed wig. The larger movements in conjunction with these smaller gestures supply the modern actor with a varied and rich palette of physical communication. When these gestures are studied and integrated into character and performance, one is never at a loss for what to do with one's hands. What follows is a description of probably the two most important— or at least most popular—uses of props for gesture: the use of the fan and the taking of snuff. Subsequently, several other types of gesture will be described. Along the way, suggestions will be made as to how or when these gestures and props may be employed. At the end of the discussion are exercises that incorporate all aspects of movement and gesture.

Using the Fan

For the gentlewoman, the primary and indispensable personal prop was, of course, the fan. The folding fan first appeared somewhere just prior to the last quarter of the century and remained in favor for the remainder of the period, once in a while being replaced with the ostrich-plumed *whisk*. Fans were made from a variety of fine fabrics and many were handpainted. A beautifully rendered fan would, undoubtedly, be elegantly and self-consciously displayed. However, the primary purpose of any fan was to provide the owner with ample opportunity for nonverbal communication and gesturing. It could be viewed as a weapon in verbal warfare and seen as an extension of a lady's personality. It could establish her mood and quite simply provide her with something "polite" to do with her hands, much as the cigarette or a glass of wine does today. It could be used either open or closed, and it could, in fact, be fluttered. However, the most common modern notion regarding the use of a fan is undermined by Edith Evans' famous contention that "the only thing you can't do with a fan is fan yourself."[9]

When it comes to the actual handling of the fan, there are two categories to consider: the actual placement of the fan when it is in repose (the positions of the fan) and the actual "language" of the fan. The positions were simply positions of rest to be utilized when the fan was not being used in conversation. The language of the fan, however, involved gesturing with the fan in ways that would punctuate or emphasize a point. Specific gestures were also designed to send nonverbal messages when not speaking or to send a contradictory one when speaking. Portraiture of the day reveals the various positions of the fan, and the later arbiters of deportment in the eighteenth century delineated positions that are

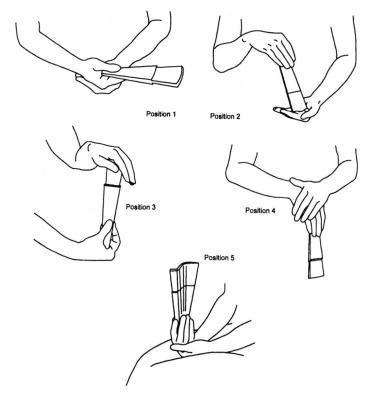

FIGURE 5-17 The Five Fan Positions © 2001 by Arthur Dirks

extremely useful to the modern actor, even if not the precise code of the Restoration era. It is these positions that will be described here. It should be noted, however, that in production, the director and actors might wish to design their own positions and common language for the fan, as historical accuracy in performance is not as important as consistency.

The Positions of the Fan

Generally, five major positions emerge. The first one has been delineated earlier within the description of standing for the gentlewoman. That is, the right hand is holding the closed fan, which is extended out over the fingers, and the left palm is facing up. The back of the right hand is laid in the palm of the left, as the arms are held in front of the bodice (just below waist level) and slightly away from the body. (See Position 1 in Figure 5-17.) When costumed, the actor will find this position to be a relaxing one, as the hands can actually rest on the fabric of the gathered folds at the waistline of the skirt. This is the most typical position and is used for standing, sitting, walking, and curtsying.

The remaining four positions, however, provide other options for the actor whereby she may bring variety to her performance. All but the final position require the fan to remain closed, and all but the final may be used for standing and sitting. In the second position, the fan is held in the right hand (also with fingers extended) and angled downward into the upturned palm of the left hand. The upper hand is slightly above waist level. (See Position 2 in Figure 5–17.)

For the third position, the fan is held in the same manner as in the second and the hands are merely turned over, or inverted, so that the left hand is atop the right. (See Position 3 in Figure 5–17.)

The fourth requires the fan to be held vertically downward with the palm of the left hand cupped over the back of the right hand. (See Position 4 in Figure 5–17.)

For the fifth position, the fan is upright and partially open. The right hand, which is holding the fan, is placed in the palm of the left, which is cupping the back of the right hand. This is a good posture for sitting and is not used when standing. (See Position 5 in Figure 5–17.)

The Language of the Fan

With respect to a language for the fan, or positions and gestures that send nonverbal messages, suggestions abound. Witty instruction comes from the pen of Joseph Addison, printed in his popular *Spectator* in 1711, in which he instructs young women in the use of the fan through his purported "academy."[10] Some of this amusing text will be cited here, as it provides a whole array of excellent suggestions for modern actors. Some of the very best instruction is given by Joan Wildeblood, who provides lists of "attitudes with the fan closed," and "attitudes with an open fan."[11] Some of her suggestions will also be provided. However, as mentioned, in production it is often sufficient to devise an original, agreed-upon language for the fan, perhaps combining suggestions from both Addison and Wildeblood.

Following are several segments of Addison's instructions to the ladies in his hypothetical academy for the use of the fan.

> When my female regiment is drawn up on array, with everyone her weapon in her hand, upon my word to *handle their fans*, each of them shakes her fan at me with a smile, then gives her right-hand woman a tap near the shoulder, then presses her lips with the extremity of her fan, then lets her arm fall in an easy motion, and stands in readiness to receive the next word of command. All of this is done with a closed fan . . .
>
> The next motion is the unfurling of the fan, in which are comprehended several little flirts and vibrations, as also gradual and deliberate openings with many voluntary fallings asunder in the fan itself . . .

Upon my giving the words to *discharge their fans*, they give one general crack that may be heard at a considerable distance when the wind sits fair . . .

There is an infinite variety of motions to be made use of in the *flutter of the fan*. There is the angry flutter, the modest flutter, the timorous flutter, the confused flutter, the merry flutter, and the amorous flutter. Not to be tedious, there is scarce any emotion in the mind which does not produce a suitable agitation in the fan; insomuch that I only see the fan of a disciplined lady, I know very well whether she laughs, frowns or blushes . . . I need not add that a fan is either a prude or a coquette, according to the nature of the person who bears it.[12]

Joan Wildeblood's suggestions for the language of the fan provide an exciting starting point for classroom or studio work, as well as for a company designing a common fan vocabulary. Some ideas with the closed fan include

(a) To the lips. (*Be quiet, we are overheard.*)
(b) Touching the right cheek. (*Yes.*)
(c) Touching the left cheek. (*No.*)
(d) Cover the left ear with the closed fan. (*Do not betray our secret.*)[13]

Some ideas she provides for the open fan include

(a) Hide the eyes behind widespread fan. (*I love you.*)
(b) Hold the opened fan over your head. (*I must avoid you.*)
(c) Slowly lower the opened fan, in the right hand, till the sticks are pointing toward the ground. (*I despise you.*)[14]

Snuff Taking

Reaching its height of popularity at the turn of the century, snuff was used by men during the early Restoration, and by both men and women from about 1700 on. Though the smoking of tobacco was also practiced, it was done typically in one's own home. Taking snuff was deemed appropriate in most social settings, and, like the fan, was used to point speech as well as to display a particularly ornate snuffbox. The tapping of the lid, the actual sniffing, and the dusting of one's hand with a handkerchief were all a part of the elaborate dance of life.

There appear to have been two methods of snuff taking during the Restoration, the latter becoming more in vogue during the eighteenth century. First, the snuffbox was carried in a vest or coat pocket and was typically spring-loaded for easy opening with one hand. The following description may be reversed if the actor is left-handed. Holding the box in the left hand, between the thumb and middle finger, the top is tapped with the second and third fingers of the right hand. The box is then opened, typically by pushing the release button with the thumb of the

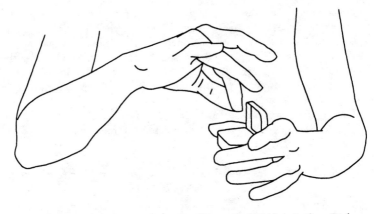

FIGURE 5–18 Hands with Snuff Box © 2001 by Arthur Dirks

hand holding the box. The snuff is removed with the right hand utilizing the thumb and the third finger. (See Figure 5–18.) For the first method, the snuff is put directly to a nostril and sniffed. For the second, the snuff is put on the back of the left hand, in the small fleshy area between the index finger and the thumb, before the hand is raised to a nostril for sniffing. (The box may be closed whenever it is comfortable during the process.) In both cases, a handkerchief is removed from a sleeve or pocket and the back of the hand is dusted. Using the right hand, the box may be returned to a pocket either before the sniffing or after.

Other Gestures for Women

The Walking Stick and the Mask

The use of two other personal props for gentlewomen must be considered: the mask and the walking cane. The cane, which was certainly used for strolling, could also be used in polite conversation, providing the owner with yet more "polite" movement for the hands. The mask was a necessary prop for all Restoration ladies, as they wore it when they did not desire to be recognized when going out. They also wore it if attending the theatre. Upon being saluted by friends, however, a lady must be sure to remove her mask. The mask could be attached to the hair, tied on, or held in place by a small mouthpiece into which the wearer would bite. Both of these props offer additional stage business for the modern actor.

A Lady's Subtle Arsenal

In addition to her use of props, the Restoration gentlewoman, and even more so, the Restoration actress, possessed a wide vocabulary of small physical gestures. It is the utilization of these smaller gestures that completes the dance of life to be enacted by the modern actor. Lyn Oxenford goes so far as to claim the following:

> The ladies preened and pranced like pigeons, drew their heads in and fluttered their eyelashes as they melted into the gentlemen's arms, and altogether showed the complete knowledge of their charms that is apparent in the newly-curled poodle.[15]

Inherent in this statement is the suggestion that the Restoration lady acquired an entire arsenal of small physicalizations that she utilized quite lavishly. Following is a list of potential gestures that can be integrated into the spoken lines, as well as into the nonverbal communication when a character is not speaking. A few examples of how they may be used are also provided for each one.

1. Especially when curls are clustered at the sides of the head, shake the curls to register agreement, disagreement, or to point a statement to which you are profoundly committed. The female fops may relish this gesture and use it extravagantly.
2. Lower the eyelids and peek from underneath. This is a particularly seductive gesture, but it can also be used for registering sarcasm or boredom.
3. "Nod" the *fontage*, which is sitting forward on the head, by letting it bounce delicately. This can suggest enthusiasm, assent, and overall good spirits. Here, too, can the fop indulge quite lavishly.
4. Elegantly and slowly shrug and lower the shoulders to draw attention to the *décolletage*. The purpose is obvious.
5. Flutter the eyelashes to register seduction, anger, amusement, or even sarcasm.
6. Although the head should not lower forward during a curtsy, a nice effect redolent with subtext may be achieved by a slight inclination to either side, including the suggestion of seduction, irony, or sneering.
7. Allow the arms to fall gracefully away from one of the fan positions and droop at the side to signify pouting or, perhaps, anger.

Other Gestures for Men

The Restoration man and actor could be equally expressive with physical gesture as the women. Following is a short list of some potential prop-initiated gestures and ones that do not require props to be employed by the men.

1. Flick at invisible bits of tobacco on a waistcoat to draw attention to particularly expensive fabric or to punctuate, for instance, disagreement or displeasure.

2. Mindlessly brush away a stray curl or lock that has fallen out of place to suggest idleness, a carefree spirit, or self-assuredness. In the hands of a fop, this motion will be used extravagantly to draw attention to the wig or, all too frequently, to punctuate a witty similitude or epigram.

3. Toy with the elaborate carving at the end of a cane while speaking to indicate a sense of detachment or boredom. If a fop, play with the ribbons and bows that may be tied to the handle.

4. Pull out the handkerchief to punctuate a well-pronounced epigram or similitude. Add a flourish to this movement to demonstrate your keen verbal and physical agility. The handkerchief may also be carried in the gesturing hand to punctuate speech throughout discourse. The fop will overuse the handkerchief and may add many flourishes in circular motions.

5. With a circular motion of the hand, flick away the long lace around the cuff, not only to draw attention to it for its own sake, but also to punctuate speech and perhaps suggest annoyance or a sense of closure.

6. If a fop, draw out a large elaborate comb from the pocket of the waistcoat and idly pull it through a few curls to signify elegance, boredom, or sarcasm or to relish a juicy bit of gossip.

7. Idly toy with a watch that hangs from the neck or that has been tucked into the pocket of a waistcoat. This may be used to suggest seduction or boredom.

Again, all of these ideas represent only potential applications for use in subtext. In theatrical production, most of these gestures can be employed with most any subtext, as will be discovered through experimentation with textual integration.

EXERCISES FOR INTEGRATING GESTURE WITH MOVEMENT AND TEXT

1. As with the previous exercises for standing, sitting, and walking, move about a room that is arranged with chairs and benches, practicing the bows, curtsies, and the nonverbal gestures, particularly the use of the fan and snuff taking. Do this first in silence. It might be helpful to post the following on a chalkboard or an easel with a tablet: "stand, pose, walk, sit, passing and formal bow, passing and formal curtsy, fan positions, language of the fan, snuff taking, cane, comb, watch, mask, cuff lace, and other nonprop gestures." Move about the room, occasionally checking the list so as to try to incorporate as many of the gestures as is possible. Meet and greet

people; sit in conversational groupings; pose to display your finery; send private messages to someone across the room; walk alone
or with someone else; and incorporate as many of the gestures as
possible, making sure that all contain a component of subtext.

2. As a group, decide on a topic for which each person is capable of
thinking of several items within the topic. Again, colors, food, music, automobiles, and the like are always typical and good choices.
As noted previously, engage in witty discourse by devising alliterative phrases based on the chosen topic, indulging in verbal battles,
gossip, witty repartee, or just idle chatter. However, at this point in
the process, begin to incorporate the gestures to point a phrase or
emphasize a point and also to send nonverbal messages to others
in the room. Continue to move about the room, stopping whenever appropriate to engage in dialogue. You may remain standing
or sit when stopping for conversation. Allow conversations to occur and evolve spontaneously. Small groups may form or the group
may converse at large. Participants may still wish to refer to the
posted list of movements and gestures.

3. Next, try the same exercise as in step 2, but memorize two or more
of the similitudes and/or epigrams from the previous exercises.
Again, do not be concerned about the literal or implied meaning in the devices, but use them to converse and engage in witty
discourse. Pay particular attention to pointing and balancing the
similitudes and epigrams with gesture. At first, the exercise may
progress quite slowly as the determinations are quite conscious.
After a time, the process will accelerate.

4. Memorize one of the following short scenes, inserting gestures at
the points noted by asterisks. Not all gestures will happen precisely
in the moment prior to the subsequent word, but may happen "on"
the word or continue into the line. Note that bows and curtsies
are already determined. It should be pointed out that this exer-
cise/scene work requires a fair amount of rehearsal. Ideally, the
scenes should be prepared and then presented to a group.

DORIMANT AND HARRIET, FROM ETHEREGE'S
MAN OF MODE

DORIMANT: (*Performing a formal bow on first phrase*) Think of making a
party, Madam; (*Rising from the bow*) love will engage. (*Taking the two steps
to the standing position*)

HARRIET: (*Performing a formal curtsy on the first line*) You make me start.
(*Rising*) I did not think to have heard love from you.*

DORIMANT: I never knew what was to have a settled ague yet,* but now
and then I have irregular fits.*

HARRIET: *Take heed!* Sickness after long health is commonly more violent and dangerous.*

DORIMANT: (Aside) *I have took the infection from her, and feel the disease now spreading in me. *(To her) Is the name of love as frightful that you dare not state it?*

HARRIET: *'Twill do little execution out of your mouth on me, *I am sure.

DORIMANT: It has been *fatal—

HARRIET: To some easy women, *but we are not all born to one destiny. I was informed you used to laugh at love *and not make it.

DORIMANT: *The time has been but now I must speak—

HARRIET: *If it be on that idle subject, I will put on my serious look, *turn my head carelessly from you, *drop my lip, *let my eyelids fall and hang half o'er my eyes—thus *—while you buzz a speech of an hour long in my ear, and I answer never a word. *Why do you not begin?

DORIMANT: *That the company may take notice how passionately I make advances of love, *and how disdainfully you receive 'em!

HARRIET: *When your love's grown strong enough to make you bear being laughed at, *I'll give you leave to trouble me with it. (A smaller formal curtsy is performed on the next line) Till then pray forbear, Sir.

BELINDA AND ARAMINTA, FROM CONGREVE'S OLD BATCHELOUR

BELINDA: (Curtsying on the first full sentence) Ay! Nay Dear—prithee good, dear sweet cousin, no more. Oh Gad, I swear you'd make one sick to hear you.*

ARAMINTA: (Curtsying during the line) Bless me! What have I said to move you thus?*

BELINDA: *Oh you have raved, talked idly, and all in Commendation of that filthy, *awkward, *two-leg'd Creature, *Man—you don't know what you said, *your Fever has transported you.

ARAMINTA: *If Love be the Fever which you mean; *Kind Heav'n avert the cure. Let me have Oil to feed that Flame and never let it be extinct, *till I my self am Ashes.*

BELINDA: There was a Whine—*O Gad I hate your horrid Fancy—*This love is the Devil and sure to be in Love is to be *possessed—Tis in the head, *Heart, *the Blood, *the—*All over—*O Gad you are quite spoil'd—I shall loath the sight of Manhood for your sake.*

ARAMINTA: *Fie, this is gross Affectation—*A little of Bellmour's company would change the scene.

BELINDA: *Filthy Fellow! *I wonder Cousin—

ARAMINTA: *I wonder Cousin you should imagine, I don't perceive you *love him.

BELINDA: *O I love your hideous Fancy! *Ha, *ha, *ha, love a Man!*

ARAMINTA: Love a Man!* Yes, yes, you would not love a Beast! (*Small formal curtsy*)

MR. PINCHWIFE AND MR. SPARKISH, FROM WYCHERLEY'S *COUNTRY WIFE*

PINCHWIFE: *What, invite your Wife to kiss Men? *Monstrous, are you not asham'd? *I will never forgive you—

SPARKISH: *Are you not asham'd, that I shou'd have more confidence in the chastity of your Family, than you have; *you must not teach me, (*Small formal bow performed on next line*) I am a man of honor, Sir, (*Rising*) though I am frank and free; I am frank, Sir—

PINCHWIFE: Very frank, Sir, *to share your Wife with your Friends.

SPARKISH: He is an *humble, *menial Friend, such as reconciles the differences of the Marriage-bed; *you know Man and Wife do not always agree, I design him for *that use, therefore wou'd have him well with my Wife.*

PINCHWIFE: A menial Friend *—you will get a great many menial Friends, by shewing Your Wife as you do.*

SPARKISH: *What then, it may be I have a *pleasure int's, as I have to *shew fine Clothes, at a Play-house the first day, and count money before poor Rogues.*

PINCHWIFE: He that shews his *wife, or *money will be in danger of having them *borrowed sometimes.

SPARKISH: *I love to be envy'd, and wou'd not marry a Wife, that I alone cou'd love; *loving alone is as dull, as *eating alone; is it not a frank age, and I am a frank Person? *and to tell you the truth, it may be I love to have *Rivals in a Wife, they make her seem to a Man still, but as a *kept Mistress; (*Small formal bow on the next line*) and so good night, for I must to Whitehall.

SCENE ANALYSIS

As with the previous three chapters, what follows is an analysis of the scene from *The Way of the World*. A portion of the scene will now be analyzed with respect to potential movement and gestural choices. The following suggestions are offered from the perspective of stage business. That is, they are theatrical in that they are chosen in order to serve as a demonstration of possible placements within the text purely for stage purposes, rather than as any representation of how they may have been used in actual life during the period. At this point, it may be beneficial for the actors to rehearse this now-familiar scene, incorporating some or all of the suggestions for movement and gesture. Another approach is to rehearse the scene utilizing one's own physical choices, inserting these in the text as indicated by placements of suggestions in the analysis. One may also desire to make all choices with respect to movement and placement of these choices.

Mirabell, Witwoud, Millamant, Mrs. Fainall, and Mincing, from Congreve's *Way of the World*

MIRABELL: (*Bowing on the first line*) You seem to be unattended, Madam—(*Rising from the bow*) You us'd to have the (*Takes the two steps to the posed standing position on the next two syllables*) Beau-mond Throng after (*Right hand falls into upturned position on the next word*) you; and a Flock of gay fine Perrukes hovering round you (*Flicks cuff lace on "you"*).

WITWOUD: (*Bows on first phrase*) Like moths about a Candle—(*Snaps to upright position*) I had (*Takes the two posing steps on "like" and "lost"*) like to have lost my (*Flicks lace over right hand to place it in posed position before the next word*) Comparison for want of (*Flicks a curl over his shoulder on next word*) breath.

MILLAMANT: (*Executes a full formal curtsy in false modesty on the first phrase*) O I have deny'd my self Airs to Day. (*Rising from the curtsy*) (*Note: Mrs. Fainall could answer with a curtsy at this time.*) I have walk'd as fast through the Crowd—

WITWOUD: (*Having taken out his snuff box on Millamant's line, he snaps it open*) As a Favourite in disgrace: (*He plucks out a bit of snuff*) and with as few Followers (*Sniffs the bit of snuff to punctuate the line*).

MILLAMANT: (*While speaking, she places her fan tip on her forehead to signify that Witwoud is behaving in a crazy manner*) Dear Mr. Witwoud, truce with your Similitudes; For I am as sick of 'em—(*Removing fan, preparing to point a similitude*)

WITWOUD: As a Phisician of a good air (*He snaps his snuff box closed*)—(*Performing a bow while speaking*) I cannot help it Madam, tho' 'tis against myself.

MILLAMANT: (*Thrusting her hands into the third fan position*) Yet again! Mincing, stand between me and his Wit (*Motioning toward Witwoud with the fan to point "Wit"*).

WITWOUD: (*Pulling out his handkerchief with much flair*) Do Mrs. Mincing, like a Skreen before a great Fire. (*Langorously dusting invisible tobacco dust from his hand)* I confess I do blaze to Day, I am too bright.

MRS. FAINALL: (*Brushing Witwoud away by using a half-opened fan, the back to Witwoud, and performing a sweeping motion)* But dear Millamant, why were you so long (*Snaps her hands to a new fan position)?*

MILLAMANT: (*Tilting her head to one shoulder, as if pouting)* Long! Lord, have I not made (*Shrugging her shoulders)* violent haste? I have ask'd every living thing I met for you; I have enquir'd after you, as (*Changing fan positions)* after a new Fashion.

WITWOUD: Madam, (*Shaking his finger at Millamant)* truce with your Similitudes—No, you met her Husband and did not ask him for her (*Flicking his cuff lace).*

MILLAMANT: (*Performing a small curtsy)* By your leave Witwoud, (*Rising)* that were like enquiring after an old Fashion, to ask a Husband for his Wife (*Shaking her curls).*

WITWOUD: Hum, a hit, a hit, a palpable hit, (*Performing a mock grave formal bow)* I confess it.

MRS. FAINALL: (*Noisily snapping her fan to a new position to get attention)* You were dress'd before I came abroad.

MILLAMANT: (*Touching her fan to the right side of her face)* Ay, that's true—(*Changing to the second fan position)* O but then I had—Mincing what had I? (*Inverting the second fan position)* Why was I so long?

MINCING: O Mem, (*Bobbing into a sharp, small curtsy while holding Millamant's train)* your Laship staid to peruse a Pecquet of Letters.

MILLAMANT: O (*Dropping her hands into standard fan position)* ay, Letters—I had Letters—I am persecuted with Letters— I (*Shaking her curls on the following two words)* hate Letters—No Body knows how to write Letters; and yet one has 'em, one does not know why—(*Pointing with her fan to her hair)* They serve one to pin up one's Hair (*Allowing her hands to float back to the standard fan position).*

WITWOUD: (*Sharply pivots away from Millamant)* Is that the way? Pray Madam, do you pin up your Hair with all your Letters? I find I must keep (*Flicking a curl away)* Copies.

MILLAMANT: (*Allowing her head to drop seductively to one side)* Only with those in verse, Mr. Witwoud. I never pin up my Hair with Prose. (*Bringing her head upright)* I fancy one's Hair wou'd not curl if it were pinn'd up with Prose. I think I try'd once Mincing.

MINCING: (*Slowly shaking her head*) O Mem, I shall never forget it.

MILLAMANT: Ay, (*Pouting her lips and shaking her head slowly in mock gravity*) poor Mincing tift and tift all morning.

MINCING: (*Holding the train in her arms, walks forward, showing her fingers to all*) 'Till I had the Cremp in my Fingers I'll vow Mem. (*Shaking her curls*) And all to no purpose. But when your Laship pins it up with Poetry, ("*Bobs*" *a little curtsy*) it sits so pleasant the next Day as any Thing, and is so pure and crips.

WITWOUD: Indeed, so (*Flicks both cuffs up*) crips?

MINCING: You're such a Critick, Mr. Witwoud.

MILLAMANT: (*Floating and pivoting to face Mirabell*) Mirabell, did not you take Exceptions last Night?—(*Moving fan to the right side of her face*) O ay, and went away—Now I think on't I'm angry—(*Moving fan to left side of face*) No now I think on't I'm pleased—(*Touching her fan to her chest*) For I believe I gave you some Pain.

MIRABELL: (*Lightly toying with the end of his walking cane*) Do's that please you?

MILLAMANT: (*Dropping hands to standard fan position*) Infinitely; I love to give Pain.

MIRABELL: (*Letting the end of his cane drop to the ground*) You wou'd affect a Cruelty which is not in your Nature; (*Stepping closer to Millamant and pivoting slightly at an attractive angle toward her*) your true Vanity is in the power of pleasing.

MILLAMANT: (*Curtsying in mock humility*) O I ask your Pardon for that—(*Rising from curtsy*) One's Cruelty is one's Power and when one parts with one's Cruelty, (*Changing fan to the fourth position*) one parts with one's Power; and when one has parted with that (*Touching tip of her fan to her chin to signal annoyance with Mirabell and to draw attention to her beauty*) I fancy one's Old and Ugly.

ACTING, TEXT, VOICE, AND MOVEMENT: A SYNTHESIS

As noted previously in this chapter, it is important that the various aspects of performing the texts of Restoration comedies be considered concurrently. Now that all aspects of movement and gesturing have been explored, it is imperative that the actor incorporate these skills with her knowledge of the texts, vocal concerns, and acting considerations. Typically, most actors or student actors attempt to do this in an ongoing manner. However, at this time it is quite beneficial to utilize the texts with which familiarity has occurred as a basis to integrate one's knowledge and acquired skills. It may be helpful to begin with any of the short solo passages found in any of the chapters and then to move on to the short scenes repeated throughout the book. After this, for the classroom or studio, it is recommended that the actors engage in more substantial scene work.

What follows is a list of questions, or the basis for analysis, that may be utilized in attempting to integrate all facets of this study of performing Restoration comedies. If beginning this work with short passages, the analysis will be correspondingly brief and all topics may not be covered. When analyzing a longer scene or applying the questions to an entire play, the questions will provide a quite comprehensive basis from which to work. When answering the following questions, it is important that the commonalities in overall aesthetic and sensibility be identified. The actor should always pay particular attention to how the text, the movement, the acting, and the use of the voice all contribute to a sense of artifice, elegance, ease, calculated casualness, flaunting, and masking, or of going too far in any of these directions when playing a false wit.

CHARACTER ANALYSIS/WORKSHEET

1. Does my character's name offer any insight into his or her objectives and desires?
2. Is she or he a true wit, a false wit, or a witless?
3. What does my character want overall?
4. Generally, what kinds of *external* behavior will my character rely on to achieve this objective?
5. Overall, how successful will my character be in executing the socially prescribed behaviors?
6. How successful is my character in masking authentic emotion?
7. How heavily does my character rely on flaunting or a sense of display?
8. How successful is my character in the battle of wits?
9. Does my character engage in a verbal love battle, raillery, the use of innocuous words to mask bawdiness or gossip, or witty repartee?
10. Does my character employ epigrams and similitudes? How are these devices structured?
11. Is there any use of double entendres?
12. Does my character engage in rant or cant?
13. In each sentence or thought unit, what are the operative words that must be emphasized? (Consider both those that convey meaning and decorative ones.)

14. Which overall effort action will my character rely on for speaking? Which ones will she or he utilize to stress operative words? Where do the changes occur?

15. How does my character utilize pitch, rhythm, and tempo changes to create meaning and highlight operative words? Where can these changes be used specifically?

16. Are there any specific vowel and consonant sounds that my character particularly likes to play? Which specific sounds can be played up in specific words and specific passages?

17. How does my character dress? Does he or she dress in the latest fashion? Does he or she scorn fashion or is he or she a slave to fashion? Is he or she excessive?

18. What effort action does my character rely primarily on as an impulse for movement? Which effort actions inform the movement in a secondary or tertiary manner?

19. How at ease is my character with the prescribed standing and sitting postures and the carriage of walking? Are there postures that my character favors?

20. Where in the text do postural changes occur?

21. How accomplished is my character with bowing or curtsying?

22. Where in the text do these occur, either the formal ones or the passing ones?

23. Does my character use a fan or take snuff? How adept is she or he in these endeavors?

24. Where in the text can these actions occur?

25. Is there occasion to use a walking stick or a mask? Where might this happen?

26. Does my character rely on any of the smaller or subtler gestures? Where can these be incorporated into the text?

NOTES

1. Some of the more notable writings addressing deportment in the Restoration are listed in Appendix B.

2. Athene Seyler and Stephen Haggard, *The Craft of Comedy* (New York: Theatre Arts, 1957), p. 74.

3. Lucy Barton, *Historic Costume for the Stage* (Boston: Walter H. Baker, 1938), p. 272.

4. Lyn Oxenford, *Playing Period Plays* (Woodstock, II: Dramatic, 1995), p. 200.

5. Ibid., p. 184.

6. Kellom Tomlinson, *The Art of Dancing Explained by Reading and Figures*, etc., 1735, Chapter 1, as quoted in J. L. Styan, *Restoration*

Comedy in Performance (Cambridge: Cambridge University Press, 1986), p. 67.

7. John Essex, *The Dancing Master; or, The Whole Art and Master of Dancing Explained,* from the French of Rameau, 1726, as quoted in Styan, p. 121.

8. Seyler and Haggard, p. 78.

9. Edith Evans, *Play and Players,* December 1976, p. 39, as quoted in Styan, p. 108.

10. Joseph Addison, *Spectator,* 27 June 1711, as quoted in Styan, p. 109.

11. Joan Wildeblood, *The Polite World: A Guide to English Manners and Deportment* (London: Davis-Poynter, 1965), pp. 219, 220.

12. Addison, as quoted in Styan, p. 109.

13. Wildeblood, p. 219.

14. Ibid., pp. 219, 220.

15. Oxenford, p. 185.

APPENDIX A
A VOCAL WARM-UP*

I. Relaxation and Breathing

Whenever possible, begin by lying on the floor on your back.

1. Whether lying or standing, concentrate on relaxing your body—identifying and eliminating as much tension as possible—and deepening your breathing. Ultimately, and ideally, the ribs should swing open as inhalation takes place; then the abdominal muscles should engage, which initiate exhalation and support the outgoing breath.

2. Activity that increases the heart rate may be employed to create a greater demand for oxygen, such as jumping jacks, running, or dancing. Fitzmaurice *tremors* are the most efficient and productive way of achieving this state and may be employed standing and/or lying down.[1] If time permits, simple relaxation will eventually allow the breathing to deepen. With either approach, attempt to send (or think) tension out of the body when you exhale.

3. Take time to observe your breathing without attempting to alter it; repeat this throughout the warm-up.

II. Major Joints and Muscles (standing or lying down)

Work major joints in a circular motion.

1. Work the ankles (by standing on one leg if doing this while standing) by drawing circles in the air with your big toe. Be sure to alternate feet.

2. Work the knees by drawing circles with each foot. Again, if executing while standing, stand on one leg and then alternate.

3. "Swivel" through the hips from front to back, side to side, and make large circles in both directions. If standing, keep knees slightly bent and your feet approximately shoulder width apart. If lying down, lift your hips off the mat by bending your knees and pressing the feet into the floor.

4. Roll the shoulders in their sockets in both directions. If lying down, lifting the shoulders toward the ceiling in a circular motion creates the same release.

5. Gently turn the chin several times from shoulder to shoulder to free the neck muscles.

6. Release the jaw by allowing it to fall open naturally.

*Cynthia Blaise, Associate Professor, Wayne State University, Detroit, Michigan

III. Alignment (standing participants should begin with step 3)
    1. If still lying down, attempt to lengthen the spine and widen the distance between your shoulder blades. Feel the support that the floor provides, the weight of your bones, and the pull of gravity.
    2. Slowly and gently come to your feet and attempt to re-create the freedom you established on the floor.
    3. Now, begin to create perfect alignment while standing. Perform a roll down and as you roll up, stack one verte-bra atop the next in an effort to lengthen the spine. This is particularly important for the neck.
    4. Your feet should be approximately shoulder width apart in a parallel position to each other. In an effort to eliminate tension, roll through the feet by placing all of the weight on the balls of your feet, then on the outsides of your feet, and finally, on your heels. Re-peat several times. Next, stand with the weight equally distributed throughout each foot. You should now be grounded.
    5. Bend your knees and then hyperextend them. Find the point of balance and *relaxed readiness* between these two extremes.
    6. The hip area should be dropped, without being pressed forward (leading with the hips) or hyperextending the curve of the spine (inordinately protruding the buttocks behind you).
    7. Reach to the ceiling with your arms to create freedom in the ribcage, one arm at a time. You should feel a release from the hip socket through the shoulders.
    8. Now, with the arms at your sides, lift and release the shoul-der area several times. As explained before, roll through the shoulders at least six times in each direction.
    9. Use the weight of your head to create a release in the mus-cles through the neck area by gently allowing the head to fall forward, then left, and then right, for at least six times.
    10. Look as far over each shoulder as possible while keeping the torso facing front, again, at least six times.
    11. Draw "figure eights" in the air with your nose.
    12. Gently massage the mandible before you shake and/or tap the jaw loose. Throughout this process, occasionally re-visit the other areas in an attempt to maintain perfect

alignment. Keep the jaw released at all times. Remember to breathe!

IV. Resonance/Vibration

1. Place one hand on the lower abdominal muscles, the other on the ribs just above the waistline, with the thumbs pointing toward the spine and the fingers pointing toward the diaphragm. This will allow you to monitor the incoming and outgoing breath and verify that support and release accompany inhalation and exhalation.

2. Determine a spot in the room to which you will direct your voice.

3. Drop the jaw; tilt the head back slightly; lift the soft palate (the back of the roof of the mouth) and allow the fuel (air) to drop into the torso.

4. The ribs and the belly (below the navel) should expand.

5. Initiate the outgoing breath with a distinct engagement of your deep abdominal muscles. Your belly will flatten in this process. Feel the ribs float back to their relaxed state as the air leaves your body.

6. Allow the outgoing breath to be bathed in vibration (voice) as it passes through your throat. Paint your point of focus in the room with the color of your voice. The sound you create should be recognizable vowels and/or diphthongs, such as those found in the following words: *lee, lay, lie, la, law, low, lou.*

7. Vary the duration, pitch, and distance of each release.

8. Check the entire torso, as well as the neck and skull, for resonance by feeling for vibration. The palms of the hands are sensitive detectors and can help you determine where vibrations exist.

9. Increase resonance by "thinking" and/or "sending" the sound/vibration to the desired area. A healthy voice has both upper-and lower-body resonance. Repeat this process many times, with as little tension as possible. Never push your voice!

V. Articulators

Articulation warm-ups should include the following:

1. For the jaw: Gently massage the jaw and then gently tap with your fist and/or shake it loose.

2. For the tongue: Stick out your tongue and point it in various directions, such as the four corners of the room. With your

tongue, paint all around the inside of your mouth. Roll or trill the tongue with an Italian *r*.

3. For the lips: Blow air through the lips in "motorboat" fashion. Blow air with and without voice. Reach and stretch all parts of the lips.

4. For the soft palate: Exaggerate the difference between a pure vowel sound (all of the air comes out of the mouth) and intense nasal resonance (all of the air passes through the nasal cavity) by reciting: "Bing-bong, ding-dong, king-kong, ling-long, ming-mong, ping-pong, sing-song, thing-thong, and zing-zong."

5. Now, with the fingertips, gently massage the jaw, temples, forehead, eye sockets, nasal passages, and larynx.

6. Drill every vowel, diphthong, and consonant sound in spoken English. The first sound in each of the following words should be exercised: *boy, Dan, fox, go, hi, jam, key, lamb, may, no, pie, quit, ray, sad, she, tea, thin, the, vow, way, yea, zoo*. You may do this by following each consonant sound with different vowels, as in: *bay, bee, by, beau, boo* or *day, Dee, die, doe, do*, and so on.

7. Tongue twisters are useful, but make sure that the voice is always well supported. For example, repeat the following several times: *baby bubble, dilly dally, giggle gaggle, kinky cookie, Lilly lolly, paper poppy, silly Sally, tilly tolly, toy boat, Topeka, mamala papala, tolika todika, badiga dabiga*, and so forth.

8. Replacing the speech sounds and tongue twisters with actual text is an excellent exercise. Pay particular attention to savoring the consonants and embellishing the vowels. Try "Get ye gone," "Ah, me unhappy," "Hie thee hither," "Oh proper stuff," "Unsex me here," "Oh, perilous mouths," "Courage, to the field," "I'll not endure it," "Oh spite! Oh Hell!" "Sir, spare your threats," "Omittance is no quittance," "Oh, horror, horror, horror," "I hate the Moor," "Fie on't, Ah Fie," "Men's vows are women's traitors," "What! Frighted with false fire!" "Are our eyes our own?" "Oh for a muse of fire," "I am possessed with an adulterate blot," "The lion dying thrusteth forth his paw," "Blush, blush thou lump of foul deformity," for example.

VI. Some Final Thoughts

1. Warming up the articulators is just as important as establishing healthy breath support. However, you do not need to be in a studio to perform these exercises. They may also

be executed in the car on your way to the theatre or to an audition, while walking to class or rehearsal, in the shower, or intermittently while applying makeup.

2. The jaw must be relaxed at all times. There should always be space between the teeth.
3. Learn to inhale without lifting your shoulders. Working in front of a mirror is always helpful.
4. Intermittent checkups throughout the rehearsal and performance are quite productive.
5. The amount of time you devote to any given exercise should be determined by your personal needs, combined with the demands of your character.
6. If you are wearing a corset, it is wise to do the breath work with your corset on, but not completely tightened. The final tightening of the corset should happen with your ribs extended and your lungs full of air.
7. A vocal warm-up should be executed with as little distraction as possible. This reinforces the concentration and focus required in performance.
8. A productive vocal warm-up should be administered with a sense of freedom, discouraging inhibiting tension whenever it presents itself.

NOTE

1. For more information on Catherine Fitzmaurice's breath and voice work, see her website at *www.fitzmauricevoice.com*.

APPENDIX B
A PARTIAL LIST OF WRITINGS ON THE ART OF DEPORTMENT IN THE RESTORATION ERA

Art of Making Love, or Rules for the Conduct of Ladies and Gallants in Their Amours, The, 1676

Character of the Beaux, The, 1676

Courtin, Antoine de, *Nouveau Traite de la Civilite Francaise*, 1676

Courtin, Antoine de, *The Rules of Civility; or, Certain Ways of Deportment Observed Amongst All Persons of Quality upon Several Occasions*, 1671

Essex, John, *The Dancing Master; or, The Whole Art and Master of Dancing Explained; And the Manner of Performing the Stops in Ball-Dancing Made Short and Ease*, from the French of M. Rameau, 1726

Gaillard, Jean, *The Compleat Gentleman; or, Directions for the Order of Youth as to Their Breeding at Home and Travelling Abroad*, 1678

Hopkins, Charles, *The Art of Love: Dedicated to the Ladies*, 1700

Muralt, *Letters Describing the Character and Customs of the English and French Nations*, 1726

Poulain, F. de la Barre, *The Woman as Good as a Man*, trans. A. L., 1677

Rameau, P., *The Dancing Master* (1725), trans. Cyril W. Beaumont, 1931

Tomlinson, Kellom, *The Art of Dancing Explained by Reading and Figures, etc.*, 1735

Vincent, Samuel, *The Young Gallant's Academy*, 1674

APPENDIX C
A PARTIAL LIST OF RESTORATION AND EIGHTEENTH-CENTURY COMEDIES

Please note that while these are not all strictly comedies of manners, most contain components or devices of the mannered comedies. Further, all provide adequate scene study for focusing on the necessary textual, vocal, and physical work to be practiced.

Aphra Behn
> *The Rover*   1677
> *The Lucky Chance*   1686

Colley Cibber
> *She Would and She Would Not*   1702
> *The Comical Lovers*   1707

William Congreve
> *The Old Batchelour*   1692
> *The Double Dealer*   1693
> *Love for Love*   1695
> *The Way of the World*   1700

John Dryden
> *Sir Martin Mar-All*   1668
> *The Mock Astrologer*   1668
> *Marriage a la Mode*   1672
> *The Assignation*   1672
> *Amphitryon*   1690

Sir George Etherege
> *She Would if She Could*   1667
> *The Man of Mode*   1676

George Farquhar
> *Love and a Bottle*   1698
> *The Constant Couple*   1699
> *The Twin Rivals*   1702
> *The Recruiting Officer*   1706
> *The Beaux' Stratagem*   1707

Thomas Otway
> *The Soldier's Fortune*   1680

Edward Ravenscroft
> *The London Cuckolds*   1681

Thomas Shadwell
> *Epsom Wells*   1672

Sir John Vanbrugh
The Relapse	1696
The Provok'd Wife	1697
The Confederacy	1705

George Villiers, Duke of Buckingham
The Chances	1666
The Rehearsal	1671

William Wycherley
The Gentleman Dancing Master	1672
Love in a Wood	1672
The Country Wife	1674
The Plain Dealer	1676

The following plays from later in the eighteenth century are also suitable for working on the values and sensibility of the comedies of manners, as both Goldsmith and Sheridan sought to recapture the scintillating brilliance of the Restoration mannered comedy.

Oliver Goldsmith
She Stoops to Conquer	1773

Richard Brinsley Sheridan
The Rivals	1775
The School for Scandal	1777

BIBLIOGRAPHY

Aries, Philippe, and Georges Duby, ed. 1989. A *History of Private Life: Passions of the Renaissance*. Trans. Arthur Goldhammer. Cambridge: Harvard University Press.

Barton, Lucy. 1938. *Historic Costume for the Stage*. Boston: Walter H. Baker.

Beaurline, L. A., and Fredson Bowers. 1967. *John Dryden: Four Comedies*. Chicago: University of Chicago Press.

Bernbaum, Ernest. 1958. *The Drama of Sensibility: A Sketch of the History of English Sentimental Comedy and Domestic Tragedy: 1696–1780*. Gloucester, MA: Peter Smith.

Brown, John Russel, and Bernard Harris, ed. 1967. *Restoration Theatre*. New York: Capricorn.

Bryant, Arthur. 1972. *The England of Charles II*. Reprint. Freeport, NY: Books for Libraries.

Cohen, Robert. 1978. *Acting Power*. Palo Alto, CA: Mayfield.

Davis, Herbert. 1967. *The Complete Plays of William Congreve*. Chicago: University of Chicago Press.

Dobree, Bonamy. 1924. *Restoration Comedy: 1660–1720*. London: Oxford University Press.

Falkus, Christopher. 1972. *The Life and Times of Charles II*. Garden City, NY: Doubleday.

Gaunt, William. 1972. *The Great Century of British Painting: Hogarth to Turner*. New York: Phaidon.

Goldhammer, Arthur, trans., and Roger Chartier, ed. 1989. A *History of Private Life: Passions of the Renaissance*. Cambridge: Belknap Press of Harvard University Press.

Grasselli, Margaret Morgan, and Pierre Rosenberg. 1984. *Watteau 1684–1721*. Washington, D.C.: National Gallery of Art.

Grout, Donald Jay. 1960. *A History of Western Music*. New York: W. W. Norton.

Gutbrie, John. 1982. *Historical Dances for the Theatre: The Pavan and the Minuet*. London: Dance Books.

Hammond, Sandra Noll. 1974. *Ballet Basics*. Palo Alto, CA: Mayfield.

Hayes, John. 1992. *British Paintings of the Sixteenth Through Nineteenth Centuries*. Washington, D.C.: National Gallery of Art, Cambridge University Press.

Latham, Robert, ed. 1985. *The Shorter Pepys*. Berkeley: University of California Press.

Laver, James, and Iris Brooke. 1964. *English Costume of the Eighteenth Century*. New York: Barnes and Noble.

Linklater, Kristin. 1992. *Freeing Shakespeare's Voice*. New York: Theatre Communications.

Loftis, John. 1977. *Sheridan and the Drama of Georgian England*. Cambridge: Harvard University Press.

Lynch, Kathleen M. 1965. *The Social Mode of Restoration Comedy*. New York: Octagon.

MacMillan, Dougald, and Howard Mumford Jones, ed. 1931. *Plays of the Restoration and Eighteenth Century As They Were Acted at the Theatres-Royal*. New York: Holt, Rinehart and Winston.

McMillin, Scott, ed. 1973. *Restoration and Eighteenth Century Comedy*. New York: W. W. Norton.

Moore, Cecil A., ed. 1933. *Twelve Famous Plays of the Restoration and Eighteenth Century*. New York: Modern Library.

Nettleton, George Henry. 1914. *English Drama of the Restoration and Eighteenth Century (1642–1780)*. New York: Macmillan.

Newlove, Jean. 1993. *Laban for Actors and Dancers*. New York: Routledge.

Nicoll, Allardyce. 1952. *A History of English Drama, 1660–1900*. Vol. 1. Cambridge: Cambridge University Press.

———. 1970. *The English Theater: A Short History*. Westport, CT: Greenwood.

Oxenford, Lyn. 1995. *Playing Period Plays*. Reprint. Woodstock, IL: Dramatic.

Palmer, John. 1962. *The Comedy of Manners*. New York: Russell & Russell.

Paulson, Ronald. 1975. *The Art of Hogarth*. New York: Phaidon.

Pearson, Hesketh. 1960. *Merry Monarch: The Life and Likeness of Charles II*. New York: Harper.

Perry, Henry Ten Eck. 1962. *The Comic Spirit in Restoration Drama*. New York: Russell & Russell.

Powell, Jocelyn. 1977. *Restoration Theater Production*. London: Routledge & Kegan Paulpic.

Price, Cecil, ed. 1973. *The Dramatic Works of Richard Brinsley Sheridan*. Oxford: Clarendon.

Randal, Don Michael, ed. 1986. *The New Harvard Dictionary of Music*. Cambridge: Belknap Press of Harvard University Press.

Saunders, Beatrice. 1970. *John Evelyn and His Times*. Oxford, NY: Pergamon.

Schneider, Ben Ross Jr. 1971. *The Ethos of Restoration Comedy*. Chicago: University of Illinois Press.

Selyer, Athene, and Stephen Haggard. 1957. *The Craft of Comedy*. New York: Theatre Arts.

Sharma, R. C. 1965. *Themes and Conventions in the Comedy of Manners*. New York: Asia.

Sichel, Marion. 1977. *Jacobean, Stuart and Restoration: Costume Reference 3*. Boston: Plays.

———. 1977. *The Eighteenth Century: Costume Reference 4*. Boston: Plays.

Squire, Geoffrey. 1974. *Dress and Society 1560–1970*. New York: Viking.

Starobinski, Jean, Philippe Duboy, Akiko Fukai, Jun I. Kanai, Toshio Horii, Janet Arnold, and Martin Kamer. 1989. *Revolution in Fashion*. New York: Abbeville.

Stonehill, Charles, ed. 1967. *The Complete Works of George Farquhar*. New York: Gordian.

Styan, J. L. 1986. *Restoration Comedy in Performance*. Cambridge: Cambridge University Press.

Summers, Montague, ed. 1967. *The Works of Aphra Behn*. New York: Phaeton.

Swain, A. E. H. 1949. *Sir John Vanbrugh*. New York: A. A. WYN.

Swedenberg, H. T. Jr., ed. 1972. *England in the Restoration and Early Eighteenth Century*. Los Angeles: University of California Press.

Von Boehn, Max. 1971. *Modes and Manners*. Vol. 3. Trans. Joan Joshua. New York: Benjamin Blom.

Vuillier, Gaston. 1972. *A History of Dancing: From the Earliest Ages to Our Own Times*. Boston: Milford House.

Weales, Gerald. 1967. *The Complete Plays of William Wycherley*. New York: University Press.

Wildeblood, Joan. 1973. *The Polite World: A Guide to English Manners and Deportment*. London: Davis-Poynter.

Wildenstein, Georges. 1960. *The Paintings of Fragonard*. New York: Phaidon.

Wilson, John Harold. 1967. *The Court Wits of the Restoration, An Introduction*. New York: Octagon.

Wood, Melusine. 1982. *Historical Dances: 12th to 19th Century*. London: Dance.

Worth, Katharine. 1992. *Sheridan & Goldsmith*. New York: St. Martin's.